MISSING
MILLIE
BENSON

The Secret Case of the Nancy Drew
Ghostwriter and Journalist

MISSING
MILLIE
BENSON

By

Julie K. Rubini

BIOGRAPHIES FOR YOUNG READERS

Ohio University Press

Athens

Ohio University Press, Athens, Ohio 45701
ohioswallow.com
© 2015 by Ohio University Press

Printed in the United States of America
Ohio University Press books are printed on acid-free paper ∞ ™

24 23 22 21 20 19 18 17 16 15   5 4 3 2 1

Frontispiece: Mildred A. Wirt. *From the private collection
of the Mildred Augustine Wirt Benson family.*

Library of Congress Cataloging-in-Publication Data
available upon request.

Contents

Author's Note

THE BOOKCASE is long gone. So too are the books that used to sit on its shelves. Their disappearance is a mystery to me. The yellow bindings beckoned me with their intriguing titles: *The Secret of the Old Clock*, *The Hidden Staircase*, *The Bungalow Mystery*.

My collection was not large. I was raised in a family with six children, and my father's was the only income. A purchased book was a rare gift. The bookmobile that arrived weekly near my home provided the solution in my quest to read about Nancy Drew's latest adventures.

I would pedal my banana-seat bike over the hot tar-covered road, with the basket carrying what I had read the week prior. I couldn't get to the library on wheels fast enough. I'd scan the shelves from floor to ceiling, hoping for a new work by Carolyn Keene. If I was lucky, I'd walk away with another volume of the mystery series in hand.

My sister and I would smuggle home-baked cookies into our room during mandatory quiet time in the afternoon. The summer breeze from the box elder tree just outside the window offered a break from the heat. We'd settle in, with our books spread across our beds, and our sun-kissed faces tucked into the pages filled with action and adventure.

I loved Nancy's ability to overcome any challenge independently and admired her ability to come and go as she pleased. Nancy reported only to her father and had a housekeeper to look after her. I envied her. I wanted to be her.

Nancy Drew created a reader out of me. Or should I say Mildred "Millie" Benson, the original writer of the Nancy Drew series, did?

As a young mother, I shared my love of reading with my children, daughters Claire and Kyle, and their younger brother Ian.

When Claire died at just ten years of age, my family, including my husband, Brad, established an organization that stages a children's book festival in her honor. Claire's Day features children's book authors and illustrators from near and far who share their passions with the thousands of families that join us every year.

The very first Claire's Day was held on May 18, 2002, in my town of Maumee, Ohio. I invited Millie, who had lived in neighboring Toledo for many years, to join us as a special guest for the day. I missed her reply phone call. Her sweet, feeble voice on my answering machine, offering her condolences, her admiration for our tribute, and her regrets in not being able to attend due to her failing health, remained with me. She died ten days later.

I did not realize that the Nancy Drew mystery stories that I grew up on were not Millie's original works. They were versions revised in 1959.

However, Millie was the original writer of the series. All of the many characterizations of Nancy that followed stemmed from the independent, feisty sleuth molded by Millie.

As I have lived all my life in northwest Ohio, I have known for some time of Millie's instrumental role with the Nancy Drew Mystery Stories. I also knew of her many years as a journalist, and enjoyed reading her various features and columns.

But there was so much of Millie's life that was a mystery to me before I was given this opportunity to research and relay her life story. Her life was filled with adventure and challenges fueled by her indomitable spirit. I came to realize that the person who should be admired for her fierce independence, spirit, and spunk is not Nancy Drew.

It's Millie.

MISSING
MILLIE
BENSON

GHOSTWRITER REAPPEARS

The Case of the Missing Ghostwriter

For the first fifty years of the series, readers of the Nancy Drew Mystery Stories, whether of the originals with the dusty blue cloth covers or the newer books with the bright yellow spines, knew that all those mysteries were written by Carolyn Keene. But who was she? No one had ever met this talented writer, seen a photograph of her face, or heard her voice on the radio. How could one of the most famous and beloved authors of suspenseful books for young people be such a mysterious figure herself?

This is where the plot thickens.

There is no Carolyn Keene. There never was.

But, like the adventurous girl detective Nancy Drew, the original writer of the series was always ready to take her readers on an exciting ride. And on May 27, 1980, she did just that—up the steps and into a

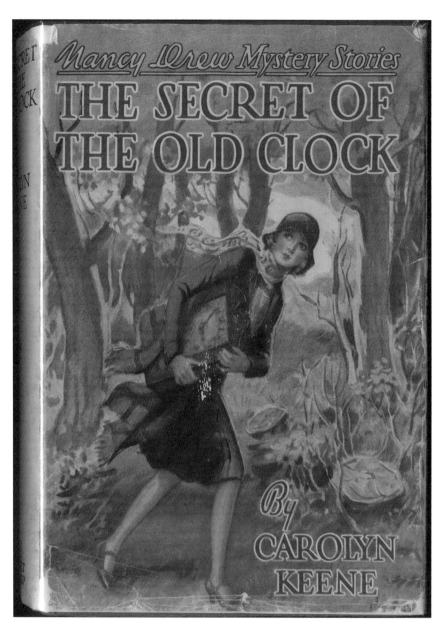

THE FIRST BOOK IN THE NANCY DREW MYSTERY STORIES,
THE SECRET OF THE OLD CLOCK, 1930

The Secret of the Old Clock, Carolyn Keene, Grosset & Dunlap. Permission granted by Penguin Group (USA) LLC.

courtroom of the United States District Court in Manhattan, and into the pages of a real life mystery to be solved as a result of a court trial.

It was a complicated trial. It involved two publishers, the businesses that print books and make them available to readers.

Both companies were fighting over the rights to publish future Nancy Drew Mystery Stories. At the end of this trial, one of the companies would win those rights; the other company would lose.

One publisher, Grosset & Dunlap, was trying to convince the judge that it should be allowed to publish new Nancy Drew Mystery Stories. That company had been making Nancy Drew's adventures available to readers since their beginning in 1930, but it had recently lost the right to publish new ones.

The other publisher, Simon & Schuster, had been chosen by the Stratemeyer **Syndicate***, the creator of the series, to publish those new Nancy Drew books. Simon & Schuster wanted the judge to decide that its company should retain the right to do so.

The Stratemeyer Syndicate was a book packaging business. The company matched writers up with books it was creating. Just as a newspaper assigns stories to writers, the Syndicate did with books. Once a writer had finished a story, the Syndicate would send the completed manuscript to a publisher. The publisher then printed the books and sold them to readers.

The Stratemeyer Syndicate and the publisher Grosset & Dunlap had been working together for almost seventy years. Then the two had parted ways over an issue they did not agree on. Grosset & Dunlap paid an amount of money, a **royalty**, to the Syndicate for every book purchased that the Syndicate had created. This meant for every Nancy Drew book that a young reader bought Grosset & Dunlap paid money to the Stratemeyer Syndicate.

Because the Nancy Drew books had always been popular, when their sales started to decline, the Syndicate blamed the publisher. Grosset & Dunlap, it felt, was not doing a good job promoting the books.

---

*A word set in boldface type indicates the first appearance within the text of a term to be defined within the glossary.

Grosset & Dunlap disagreed.[1] So the Syndicate signed a contract with another publisher, Simon & Schuster.

Because Grosset & Dunlap was not happy with the Stratemeyer Syndicate's choice to use another publisher for the Nancy Drew books, the company filed a lawsuit to get those rights back. To strengthen its case, Grosset & Dunlap brought in a special witness.

That move revealed the trial's true mystery—who was the original writer of the series? That special witness. The former **ghostwriter**.

TEMPERATURES had been quite hot in New York City for the days leading up to the trial. Yet the key witness was as cool as she could be in her powder blue pantsuit.

She was a small woman in her seventies, barely five feet tall, with short, graying hair that reflected her age. Steely eyes with a hint of whimsy peered through her round glasses, which sat firmly on her prominent nose. Her small mouth turned up at the corners, as if she were holding on to a secret.

She was.

As she walked up the many stairs of the courthouse that day, perhaps the witness was thinking about how the secret that very few people knew was about to come out. Maybe she was thinking about the late Edward Stratemeyer, who had formed the Stratemeyer Syndicate in 1905.[2] Mr. Stratemeyer had asked her to write the first three Nancy Drew books after creating an outline, a writing guide, for her.

Maybe she was thinking that someone else was getting credit for her writing and she was ready to speak out about it.

The witness may have been thinking about many years before, when, as a young writer just out of college, she wrote her first Nancy Drew book. She had been happy to accept the flat fee, or one-time payment, for each book that she wrote for Mr. Stratemeyer even if it meant that her real name wouldn't appear on the book cover. Writing for the Stratemeyer Syndicate might open other doors for her, she might have thought.

Now, fifty years later, this former ghostwriter for the Stratemeyer Syndicate was to serve as a witness for this important trial.

The witness entered the courtroom. As she was still very active, despite her senior citizen status, the long walk up the aisle didn't bother her one bit. What probably caused her more concern were the questions that she would be asked. The expectation was that she would not be able to prove that she was the original writer of the Nancy Drew series, known only as Carolyn Keene.

Once her secret came out, her life could change.

EDWARD Stratemeyer had developed his plan for making books based on his own experiences as a ghostwriter for a publisher of **story papers**. Like his previous employer, Edward created the characters and the plot. He then developed an outline, and relied upon one of a variety of writers to pen each story. Several writers could be working on the same series, but none of them would ever be known as the author.

As a ghostwriter, Edward wrote stories using different names. These names are called **pseudonyms**. So, Edward created pseudonyms for the various series that he began to develop. One of these was the pseudonym of Carolyn Keene for the writers of the Nancy Drew Mystery Stories.[3]

Edward died on May 10, 1930, just twelve days after the first three books in the Nancy Drew series were released to young readers. After his death, his daughters, Edna Stratemeyer and Harriet Stratemeyer Adams, took over the business.[4]

Harriet Stratemeyer Adams was eighty-seven years old at the time of the trial. She had contracted two years previously with Simon & Schuster to publish new books, including the Nancy Drew series, produced by the Syndicate. And, as a result, Grosset & Dunlap sued Gulf & Western, the **parent company** of Simon & Schuster. A portion of the trial involved figuring out who actually owned the Nancy Drew books. In order to solve that mystery, the judge needed to know the terms of the agreement between the individual who created the outlines, plots, and characters and the person who actually wrote the books.[5]

The former ghostwriter knew that she was an important witness for Grosset & Dunlap. Her testimony, what she said while in the witness stand, could make a difference as to which company would continue to publish the beloved Nancy Drew books.

As she was introduced to the witness, Harriet said, "I thought that you were dead."[6]

Harriet had not seen the former ghostwriter in years. And Harriet had reason to be concerned about the other woman's appearance in court. For Harriet had publicly claimed that *she* had written all of the Nancy Drew Mystery Stories.

ABOUT one month prior to the trial, fans of the Nancy Drew series were focused on something else. The literary world was about to pay tribute to the fiftieth anniversary of the release of the first Nancy Drew book. Harriet Stratemeyer Adams was enjoying the spotlight. She was being celebrated as the author of the series by *Time* magazine.[7] A mystery-theme party hosted by Simon & Schuster, complete with a cave entrance filled with prerecorded screams and party-favor flashlights, was thrown in Harriet's honor.[8]

You can imagine Harriet's surprise when this woman, contracted by her father to write the very first volumes of Nancy Drew some fifty years earlier, showed up at the trial.

So who was this mystery witness?

The trial's attorneys were about to crack the case.

Mildred "Millie" Augustine Wirt Benson was her name.

Millie was the original ghostwriter of the well-loved series. She appeared in court to testify to this fact. Millie was there to shed light on the mystery of who had actually written the original Nancy Drew books. The children's book writer was not only alive and well, but at seventy-four years old she had a quite a story to tell.

It had been over twenty years since Millie and the Stratemeyers had parted ways, but Millie felt it was time to set the record straight.

Millie, so much like the independent and no-nonsense character Nancy Drew, took the stand. She was shown a number of documents by the lawyer for Grosset & Dunlap. These included work releases signed by Millie that documented that she had agreed to write the

THE STRATEMEYER SYNDICATE, GHOSTWRITERS, AND RIGHTS

EDWARD STRATEMEYER began his career as a writer. He became a very successful juvenile fiction author, especially of stories for boys. In 1893, he had forty-nine dime novels published! Many of these books were published by a company called Street & Smith.

While working for Street & Smith, Edward learned how the company employed ghostwriters to write under pseudonyms. The dime novels the authors were assigned to write featured characters developed and owned by Street & Smith.[9]

When Edward formed his own company in 1905, the Stratemeyer Syndicate, he used similar techniques to keep up with the demand for the various series he had created. He hired writers to follow the outlines he created for his books. These writers agreed to a flat fee for payment. They did not receive any royalties, or percentages based on book sales.[10]

The benefits to the arrangement for the Syndicate included control of the characters and storylines. Since one pseudonym was used for each series, one author's name was consistently attached to the series, even if the actual writer changed.

By signing a contract, a writer agreed not to use the Syndicate's pseudonym in any other way. The writer also knew that he or she would not receive any royalties—not only those based on a percentage of the book sales, but those from movie or merchandising sales, as well. The advantages for a writer under this agreement was the **lucrative** flat payment and the possibility of writing more stories for the Syndicate.

MILLIE AND HER BOOKS

Toledo Blade Historical File, © *The Blade*

books. Millie described how Edward Stratemeyer had provided her with an outline for each of the first three books.

Grosset & Dunlap liked this spunky young detective and ordered more books in the series.

And more Millie wrote, penning twenty-three of the first thirty books in the original Nancy Drew series.

After Millie's testimony for the plaintiff, it was Harriet's turn for the defense.

Even after being presented with the evidence otherwise, Harriet still insisted, "but I actually did all the writing."[11] She became so upset after her testimony that she fell out of the witness chair.[12]

The two-week trial ended. Grosset & Dunlap lost. The judge ruled that the Stratemeyer Syndicate had the right to choose which publisher would take Nancy Drew into the future—no matter who had created or written about her in the past.[13] The Syndicate made its choice. Future Nancy Drew books would be published by Simon & Schuster.

And, as a result of the trial, the original writer of the Nancy Drew books was officially revealed.

That person was Millie Benson.

NANCY Drew stories always ended a chapter with a "holding point." This is something that made you wonder and want to keep turning the pages, even though Mom had told you several times over it was past your bedtime.[14]

So here you go . . .

Where did this mysterious writer come from? Where had she been all these years? And why is it that, even after the trial confirmed her identity as the original writer of the Nancy Drew series, she was not publicly recognized until 1993?

Get your flashlights out. Let's get on to solving the many mysteries of Millie.

DID YOU KNOW?

Pseudonyms: Did you know that several famous female writers wrote under male pseudonyms? Charlotte Brontë published *Jane Eyre* under the name Currer Bell and her sister Emily published *Wuthering Heights* under the name Ellis Bell. Millie wrote as both Don Palmer and Frank Bell.

LITTLE LADORA GIRL WITH BIG DREAMS

The Case of the Wandering Feet

N ANCY DREW and Penny Parker were two of the many characters Millie shared with the world. They were known to be quick on their feet. So was Millie.

Let's start with her baby shoes. They say a lot about her. Silky white with blue ribbons for her tiny feet. Blue was the color for little girls up until the 1940s.[1] The soles, the bottom of the shoes, were all marred and scuffed. They reflect her busy personality, even at this early age. This little girl was destined to go places.

Born on July 10, 1905, at a healthy nine pounds, Millie Augustine soon toddled around her family home in Ladora, Iowa. Ladora is about eighty miles from the capital of Des Moines. Beautiful rolling fields planted with corn, beans, and oats surrounded the town. Cattle on neighboring farms grazed in the fields and horses galloped in their

LADORA, IOWA, SEPTEMBER 1912
Pioneer Heritage Resource Library, Marengo, Iowa

pastures at the sight of the occasional visitor. The Rock Island Railroad line was built in the late 1860s and ran alongside the town. The railroad encouraged the growth of Ladora, as it allowed for the shipment of cattle and grain raised in the area.

Millie couldn't wait to start school. Beginning at the age of five, Millie skipped off to school. Her older brother, Mel, was always with her on the five-block journey.

As she grew older, in the warm summer months, Millie would saunter out to the front porch where she could watch her world go by. It was from here that Millie would see her father and mother drive off in his horse-drawn wagon. They were headed to his medical practice on the second floor of the Pike General Store just up the street. Ladora's five hundred residents counted on her father to take care of them, from birthing babies to performing surgeries.

Just up the way she could see the Ladora Savings Bank being built. The building, with its many tall windows and majestic columns, rose to greet future customers. Over a thousand people from the area attended the dedication ceremony on July 26, 1920. Millie's family was likely there, as her father served on the bank's board. The townspeople marveled at the marble counters, the wooden floors, and the huge vault. The indoor restrooms attracted quite a bit of attention too!

In the winter Millie likely would sit in the front parlor room at home, her feet in stockings and laced boots. Perhaps she was listening to her father talk about his support of Republican President William Howard Taft. Her mother might have been playing the piano in the background. Both her father's interest in politics and her mother's musical talents influenced her as she grew up.

Her father, Jasper L. "J. L." Augustine, was born in 1868, the son of a "forty-niner," one who traveled to California in 1849 after the discovery of gold. J. L.'s father, Peter Augustine, had traveled three times from Iowa to California in search of his fortune. His mother, Jennie, had always waited for Peter to return to their homestead in Agency City, Iowa. J. L. attended public schools in his hometown, and proved to be an excellent student. After high school J. L. attended the State University of Iowa (now the University of Iowa), graduating with a medical degree in 1893.[2]

Millie's father moved to Ladora after graduation, where he set up his medical practice and became quite involved in the town. J. L.'s community service included his roles on the boards of the Ladora Savings Bank and the Millersburg Savings Bank. J. L. was also a member of the Ladora Improvement Company, which helped develop the growth of the town.[3]

A young woman whose family had purchased farmland adjacent to Ladora caught the new doctor's eye. Her name was Lillian V. Matteson. Her parents, Elias and Emily, had migrated from Vermont to Iowa in 1882. Lillian's father was a farmer who had operated a sawmill in Vermont before moving to Iowa. Once settled in Ladora, he estab-

MILDRED "MILLIE" AUGUSTINE ON THE FRONT PORCH OF HER
FAMILY HOME, 1915

lished a successful farming operation. Elias was also conservative in his
political views and community-minded. He likely was impressed with
young J. L. Augustine when he came to call on his daughter, Lillian.

And so it was that young Dr. J. L. Augustine married Lillian V. Matteson in June 1897. Their first child, Melville "Mel," was born in 1898,
and Millie followed in 1905. As the children grew older, Lillian took on
the role of her husband's assistant in his medical office. She was known
as "Grandma Doctor" within the family.[4]

Her parents were very busy with her father's medical practice. As a
result, Millie grew up with "a freedom that most children don't have

MILLIE AND HER OLDER BROTHER, MEL

From the private collection of the Mildred Augustine Wirt Benson family

now." Millie's footwear at this stage included roller skates and comfortable shoes to play basketball in.[5]

Lillian created a scrapbook for Millie during her childhood years. On one page, Lillian paid tribute to the many hours Millie played with paper dolls. She even drew a picture of Millie and her creations.

Years later Millie would write that the countless hours playing with the paper dolls and making up stories had a benefit. "It taught me the very beginning of story creation and actual writing."[6]

A china doll and paper dolls were the only feminine toys she had, for her family recalls her as not being a "girly-girl."

Millie played games with her brother, who tried to scare her by jumping out from a hedge of bushes on their property. Millie didn't flinch. Nothing scared her.[7] And she always felt that girls should be able to do the same things as boys.[8]

Millie loved to read, claiming that she "read every book in the town."[9] The nearest public library was in Marengo, seven miles away. It might as well have been a hundred. Due to a lack of transportation, she never visited the library. Instead Millie borrowed books from neighbors and the local high school library. "I liked action and mysteries."[10] She also loved *St. Nicholas*, a popular monthly magazine for children.

Every month Millie would have high-tailed it up to the Ladora post office, just two blocks up the street, in her laced shoes and dresses made by her mother. She couldn't wait for the newest issue of *St. Nicholas* magazine to arrive.

Millie would sift through the pages filled with action, adventure, and even a hint of romance. She would daydream over ads for products of interest to children and their parents, including Fairy Soap for five cents. The pages were filled with beautiful illustrations and educational articles too.

A new department of the magazine created in 1899 set Millie on her course as a writer. The *St. Nicholas* League offered subscribers a chance to send stories to the magazine and to win recognition for their efforts. Millie submitted a story titled "The Courtesy," which was published in the June 1919 issue of *St. Nicholas*. The issue's "Competition

A PROVING GROUND FOR WRITERS

ST. NICHOLAS was *the* magazine for children and, often, their parents.[11] The magazine was published between 1873 and 1940.

Many famous writers wrote for the magazine, including Mark Twain, Rudyard Kipling, and Henry Wadsworth Longfellow. Young readers who, like Millie, sent stories through the *St. Nicholas* League include such famous authors as F. Scott Fitzgerald, E. B. White, and Edna St. Vincent Millay.

No. 232" under the prose category lists Silver Badge winner Mildred Augustine, age thirteen, of Iowa.

A writer was born.

Or, at least, a published writer.

As Millie offered years later, "I've written since the time that I was able to walk on my feet."[12]

Her mother supported her in her aspirations, but her father laughed at her and told her that he thought it would be difficult to make a living at writing. Dr. Augustine hoped that she would follow in his footsteps in the medical profession. Millie felt otherwise. "When I made up my mind to do something I did it."[13]

Millie continued to submit stories to *St. Nicholas* and other publications while living in Ladora. She would walk down to the post office to see if a letter had arrived from a publisher accepting her work.

Millie was not quite seventeen when she became one of four graduates from Ladora High in June 1922. She had taken summer courses in Iowa City in order to complete her high school education early.[14]

ST. NICHOLAS

Vol. XLVI   JUNE, 1919   No. 8

Yvette of the Kind Heart

By Violet Maxwell.

Yvette was a little girl who lived in a village in Normandy. She was not very beautiful to look at—her figure was long and gangling, and she had a round, freckled face, with a turned-up nose and two little twinkling green eyes and a wide mouth that was always grinning. But "Beauty is as Beauty does," and everybody loved Yvette, for she had a kind heart.

Yvette attended the village school, but alas! though she had never missed a day's attendance since she was six, and she was now thirteen going on fourteen, she had never got further in her tables than $4 \times 7 = 28$! The schoolmaster was in despair. Although he, too, loved Yvette for her kind heart, he realized that he would never make a scholar of her; so after much pondering, he went to Yvette's parents and laid the matter before them.

Yvette was clearly not cut out for book-learning! But even though not destined to be a scholar, there were several other careers which she might follow: she might become a dairymaid, and earn fame and fortune by the superiority of her cheeses; she might become a cook, and invent a new sauce; and again, she might become a farmer's wife, with round-faced children, and raise chickens and turkeys. All these careers were open to her, but one thing was clear—it was waste of time for Yvette to remain at school.

Yvette's good parents saw the truth of the schoolmaster's argument, and decided to apprentice their little daughter to a farmer.

Now, by far the wealthiest farmer in that part of the country was one "Farmer Fernagui," who owned the biggest cider-farm in all Normandy. He employed many lads and lasses in his dairies, in the kitchen, in the stables, and in the fields. Also, he made life easy for his farm-hands, gave them plenty of jollity and good things to eat, nor did he work them too hard.

Of fallen flow'rs; not yet the trees are bare:
It is the time when orchards bloom—the spring!
Half hid by blossoms white, like foaming seas
  That flash and sparkle in the evening gloom,
All gnarled and roughened stand the apple-trees;
  Across the grass, grotesque, their shadows loom.
What say these tokens? Seek ye more than these?
  It is the Spring—the time when orchards bloom!

"HEADING FOR JUNE." BY ELIZABETH E. CLARKE, AGE 15.
(HONOR MEMBER.)

THE COURTESY
BY MILDRED AUGUSTINE (AGE 13)
(*Silver Badge*)

MRS. GARDNER sat gazing out of the window. In her lap lay a letter. The door opened and her daughter Andrea entered the room. Mrs. Gardner, smiling faintly, said, "I have received a letter from Aunt Jane, who will arrive next week to spend the winter with us." For a moment Andrea was too surprised to speak. Then she burst into tears.

A week later Aunt Jane arrived, parrot, umbrella, baggage, and all. She was even worse than Andrea had imagined. She breakfasted in bed, grumbled at everything, was courteous to no one, and was, in short, as Andrea declared, "a perfect grouch."

As time passed, matters grew worse. The parrot screeched incessantly, and the house was in a constant uproar.

Several weeks after her arrival, Aunt Jane overheard a conversation that caused her much thought. Coming noiselessly past Andrea's room, she heard Andrea clearly say: "Aunt Jane thinks that we should do nothing but wait on her and show her every courtesy, while she just bosses and grumbles. For my part, I think that courtesy is as much her duty as ours. If only she were pleasant, it would be much easier for us to be courteous to her."

Aunt Jane silently entered her room.

Next morning the Gardners were surprised to find Aunt Jane down for breakfast. Later, she helped wash the dishes without even grumbling.

Weeks passed. Aunt Jane became so helpful and cheerful it was a pleasure to have her around.

When spring came, the Gardners wanted her to remain, but, declining, she announced her intention of traveling, providing Andrea would accompany her. Andrea—not from courtesy, but because she really liked Aunt Jane—accepted.

No one except Aunt Jane knew, and she never told, that it was Andrea who had first shown her the need for true courtesy.

WHEN BOUGHS ARE BARE
BY KATHERINE SMITH (AGE 15)
(*Honor Member*)

WHEN winter winds their chill blasts blow,
And on the ground are ice and snow,
When all is still, and everywhere
The great trees wave their branches bare,
What gazer on this cheerless scene
Could picture the same forest *green?*
Could fancy birds among the trees,
And bright leaves nodding in the breeze?

O reader, when your heart is sad,
When nothing seems to make you glad,
When, "Everything goes wrong," you say,
And "Nothing seems worth while to-day,"
Just try to look ahead, and smile.
Be patient for a little while!

When your heart 's filled with grief and care,
Think of the trees whose boughs are bare.
Just as the winter months are brief,
So is the time of pain and grief!
And just as comes the budding spring
With joy and life for everything,
So to you will come happier days,
Sent by the One we love and praise!

A COURTESY
BY NORMAN MACY (AGE 12)

AN old woman somewhat bent with age stood by a turnstile in a subway station buying a ticket. She was carrying a great many bundles in her arms, and was obliged to set them down in order to find her pocketbook.

While the old woman was slowly gathering up her bundles, a middle-aged woman came hurrying down the long corridor toward her. A train was just pulling into the station. The younger woman dropped her ready fare into the box and started to go through, but on account of the old woman's bundles being in the way, she could not.

"Pardon me," she said to the old woman, "but I am in a great hurry to get that train; may I pass through?"

"MY FAVORITE SUBJECT." BY LYMAN BAKER, AGE 13.

"MY FAVORITE SUBJECT." BY ELIZABETH BURTNER, AGE 13.

MILDRED'S FIRST PUBLISHED WORK
Special Collections, The University of Iowa Libraries

Millie's wandering feet were ready to move on and out of Ladora. But did she really leave Ladora behind? She told a reporter years later that "the flavor of a small town stays with you all your life."[15]

That may be true, but Millie's desire to follow her dream took her away from Ladora and eventually to many cities that she only imagined seeing as a child. So where did her feet take her next? Where did her writing?

DID YOU KNOW?

Elwyn Brooks "E. B." White not only wrote *Charlotte's Web* and *Stuart Little,* but was also the coauthor of the guide to writing style, *The Elements of Style,* also known as "Strunk & White."

COLLEGE DAYS

The Case of the Hawkeye

So now your room is silent.
The whole house seems silent too;
Every object which confronts me
Seems incomplete without you.

Yes, your silent room, it haunts me
Every garment left behind
Have memories from which bring a tear
For the loved one I cannot find.

—*Lillian Augustine, "Mildred's Room"*[1]

LILLIAN MISSED her daughter when she left Ladora for the campus of the University of Iowa[2] in Iowa City. As you are about to learn, Millie dove right in to her college experiences. Literally.

Millie's choice of college might have been determined by several factors. Perhaps her father wanted her to attend his **alma mater**. Maybe Lillian wanted her daughter close to home. Or maybe Millie was impressed that the University of Iowa was the first public university to admit men and women on an equal basis.

STUDENTS LEAVING THE HALL OF LIBERAL ARTS ON THE UNIVERSITY OF IOWA CAMPUS, 1920

Maybe the college's journalism class offerings that began in 1915 appealed to this blossoming writer.[3] Most of all, the campus newspaper may have had a role in her choice. The *Daily Iowan,* the first campus newspaper west of the Mississippi, had ties to the United Press and offered students practical experience. The newspaper was written, edited, and managed by students.

Millie became a University of Iowa Hawkeye.

Students can still be seen today reading the *Daily Iowan,* now one of the largest student newspapers in the country. For an avid reader like Millie, the paper served as a great resource as well.

Millie likely picked up a copy of the September 21, 1922, edition on the first day of registration on campus. The paper announced that the

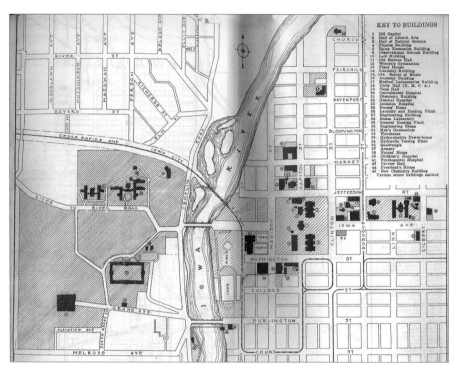

UNIVERSITY OF IOWA CAMPUS MAP, 1922–23

enrollment was expected to exceed the 5,980 students from the year prior. Millie may have been quite excited by the number of students. The student population was over ten times that of Ladora!

After completing registration, Millie walked to Currier Hall and settled into room 1573, her home for her freshman year.[4] She may have kicked off her shoes and sat on her new bed, reading the rest of the *Daily Iowan.*

Page fifteen of the paper featured a story on the progress of several buildings on campus. Work on the focal point of the university, the Iowa Old Capitol Building, with its golden dome, was to be completed

OLD CAPITOL BUILDING ON THE UNIVERSITY OF IOWA CAMPUS
University Archives, The University of Iowa Libraries. Copyright 2013 the University of
Iowa. All rights reserved.

that fall. The building had been the original seat of Iowa state government until the capital moved to Des Moines in 1857.[5]

Perhaps of greater interest to Millie in the article was the notice
that a new library building was to be built on campus. Millie would
simply have to walk across campus to have access to as many books as
her heart desired. No more borrowing books from neighbors!

Stores in Iowa City welcomed students back through their advertisements in the paper. The Lorenz Brothers Boot Shop promoted new
strap-style shoes for college girls. Millie could hop on a streetcar that ran
along Washington Street to visit the new Ritestyle Shop, which featured
the frock, a long dress that covered young ladies from neck to ankle.[6]

Millie likely attended the Women's Athletic Association meeting for freshmen women announced in the paper. Membership in the organization resulted from participating in, or making, various sports teams. Points were given based on activity level. Only twelve women had ever earned an "I" sweater based on the accumulation of a thousand points. Millie, being competitive in nature, probably had her eyes set on one of those sweaters.

Millie was an active participant in women's sports. She was one of twelve members of the freshman soccer team and a right guard on the freshman basketball team. She was a substitute on the women's swim team, known as the Seals Club.

As the Seals Club was a highly competitive team, young women interested in being a Seal had to meet a number of requirements. These included being able to swim the length of the pool in eighteen seconds, plunge twenty-five feet, and have good form for three swim strokes and three dives. Millie became a full-fledged member of the team her sophomore year. Both a strong swimmer and a high diver, Millie swam nearly every day for most of her life.

An exhibition at the "Big Dipper," the Iowa City municipal pool, pitted members of the Eels Club, the university men's swim team, against female swimmers. Millie's personal scrapbook included a newspaper clipping about one such event, a mixed relay event. Millie beat the captain of the men's 1923–24 swim team in the contest![7]

The headline of the October 15, 1922, edition of the *Daily Iowan* read, "Parkin Stars as Hawkeyes Beat Yale 6–0." Yale had never before lost to a western team in the Yale Bowl.[8]

What Millie might have found just as exciting was a **sidebar** in much smaller print. It stated that the *Iowan* had created a new speed record in getting the news of the victory from Yale to the paper's readers. The announcement came "from the press two minutes after the final flash from the United Press was received at the *Iowan* office."

Extracurricular activities were also covered in the paper. One of Millie's favorites during her time at the university (she completed her

Seals Club

Cox, McGovney, Gregg, Richter, Larren
Green, Kenyon, Benner, Starbuck, Klenze
Doornink, Acuff, Quiner, Spencer, Augustine
Prunty, Buhler, McGarvey, Kay, Fiske, Byrne

FACULTY MEMBERS

LOUISE BOILLIN	CHARLOTTE MacDOUGALL	MARION SCHWOB
ELSE BOCKSTRUCK	HELEN SAUM	MIRIAM TAYLOR

ACTIVE MEMBERS

MILDRED AUGUSTINE	ANNE DOORNINK	BEATRICE McGARVEY
AMY L. BENNER	CHARLOTTE FISK	MARGARITA McGOVNEY
GLADYS BROOKER	DORIS GREEN	ESTHER RAWLINS
MARJORIE BUHLER	MARJORIE KAY	CATHERINE RICHTER
EVELYN BYRNE	MILDRED KENYON	EMILY RUSSELL
ELEANOR CHASE	CLARA LARSEN	HELEN SPENCER
SARA COX		HELEN STARBUCK

PLEDGES

LUCELIA ACUFF	VIRGINIA GREGG	EVA PRUNTY
MARGERY COREY	FRANCES HALE	MYRNA WALDEN
	LOIS KLENZE	

MILDRED AUGUSTINE IN THE SEALS CLUB
(upper photo: second row, far right; lower photo: first row, far left)

From the University of Iowa *Hawkeye*, 1925. University Archives, The University of Iowa Libraries. Copyright 2013 the University of Iowa. All rights reserved..

MILDRED AUGUSTINE, MID-DIVE INTO THE IOWA RIVER

undergraduate degree in just three years!) was the Cosmopolitan Club. The club sought to encourage friendship and respect among men and women of all nationalities. During Millie's freshman year, eleven nations were represented in the university's chapter, including Hawaii. In 1922, Hawaii was still an independent country; it became a state in 1959.

The club staged various events to create an awareness of the different cultures and talents of its members. Millie had a unique musical skill. She played the xylophone. She not only played that instrument, she played it with two sticks (known as mallets) in each hand. Usually a xylophonist uses one in each hand. She must have been quite a sight during the international nights staged by the club!

Millie was also involved in the Athena Literary Society, the University Orchestra, Theta Sigma Phi journalism sorority, and the *Hawkeye* yearbook. She was also the president of the Matrices, an organization for young women interested in journalism.

Millie had to have been excited by the newly formed journalism program at the university that offered such courses as Reporting, News Editing, Writing for Magazines, and Problems in Journalism.[9]

Newspaper publishers throughout Iowa felt that the craft of writing for a newspaper could only be learned by actually writing for one. The University of Iowa officials overcame these concerns by linking what was taught in the classroom with actual experience in working for the *Daily Iowan*. The *Daily Iowan* was published six mornings a week and, most significantly, its staff was made up of students enrolled in the journalism classes.[10]

The editor-in-chief of the newspaper during Millie's freshman year was senior George H. Gallup Jr. He had many plans for the newspaper, including using national news from the United Press and creating a separate sports page.

Mr. Gallup completed his undergraduate degree in political science at the university in 1923. He obtained his master's and, ultimately, his PhD in psychology. Gallup also taught journalism courses at the university. During this time he began work on creating surveys for large audiences and then compiling the information. He was creating the foundation for the **Gallup Poll**, known for its research in the gathering of **statistics**.[11]

Millie's lack of fear served her well as she interviewed for a student staff position with the newspaper. She was hired to work for the *Daily Iowan* her sophomore year.

Millie the writer was on her way.

The headline of the June 10, 1925, issue of the *Daily Iowan* read, "Commencement Sees Exit of Largest Graduating Class."

Millie Augustine was one of the graduates.

GEORGE GALLUP JR. AND HIS FAMOUS POLL

THE SUMMER before his senior year at the University of Iowa, George Gallup Jr., along with fifty other students, worked for the *St. Louis Post-Dispatch*. George's job involved knocking on the doors of the city's fifty thousand residents and asking what they liked and didn't like about the newspaper. After that very hot summer, George determined there had to be a much easier way to collect that information. Basing his idea on the theories of mathematician Jakob Bernoulli, George proposed that a random selection of households in St. Louis would provide the same results as questioning everyone in the entire city.

George went on to form the American Institute of Public Opinion. Newspapers would print his surveys, called Gallup Polls, to gather public opinion. Eventually his polls were used to predict the outcome of political campaign contests.[12]

Here is an example of how a survey sampling works. Your school could ask every student in the sixth, seventh, and eighth grades how each student liked the cafeteria food. That might be a lot of students to ask! Your school could obtain the same results if it randomly drew names, making sure to keep the same proportion of girls to boys as in each class.

GEORGE GALLUP JR.

Courtesy of Drake University Archives and Special Collections

Daily Iowan Staff

Gardiner, Roach, Carter, Swenson, Tiss, Starzl, Sheldon, D. Miller, Hughes, Easter
Huebsch, Cuffey, Evans, Lane, Moeller, A. Miller, Wolters, Fairall, Vanderburg, Corey
Fuller, Maxwell, Long, Lazell, Allenson, Petersburger, Houston, Orr, Mills
Maggard, Stein, Wilson, Wade, Cutting, Hoeye, Rule, Brown, Kelleher, Lemley, Heffner
Engle, Herzer, Chase, Evans, Sinn, Coffey, Samuelson, Critz, Augustine, Russell

PUBLISHED for the first time in its history in its own plant, the *Daily Iowan*, official student newspaper of the University, was enlarged to an eight-column, eight page daily this year, printed every morning except Monday. Besides the enlargement in size, the *Iowan* became a member of the Associated Press, recognized as the world's greatest news service.

Seventy-five reporters from the University classes in journalism were employed in covering the news of the University campus and the city. It was also the first time in its history that the *Iowan* covered the news of Iowa City in a special department. The *Iowan* has full equipment consisting of presses, linotypes, type, and other equipment incidental to a newspaper office.

Offices for several of the University publications were provided in the *Iowan* building. All campus publications were organized under the graduate editor and business manager plan as used by several leading universities. George H. Gallup is graduate editor while Loren D. Upton is general manager of the Daily Iowan Publishing Company.

Besides being practically doubled in size the *Iowan* is being printed for twelve months per year, one of three college newspapers in the United States on a twelve months basis. The *Iowan* is one of two college newspapers in the United States which have a full leased wire service of the Associated Press. The *Iowan*, besides publishing its regular morning paper, has published "extras" on many occasions. The story of each football game is printed in an extra which makes its appearance on the street within a few minutes after the final whistle blows on the playing field.

The *Iowan* offers opportunity for students in journalism to secure practical training in newspaper work. The editors and reporters all do their work as part of their University courses, supplementing sound theories of the class room with the practical experience on a newspaper. The *Iowan* editor and business manager are elected by the *Iowan* board of trustees composed of faculty members and undergraduates. This board also directs the policy of the paper and holds the same relation that such boards do to other newspapers. The editor and business manager each selects and controls his own staff.

MILDRED AUGUSTINE ON THE *DAILY IOWAN* STAFF
(first row, second from right)

From the University of Iowa *Hawkeye*, 1925. University Archives, The University of Iowa Libraries.. Copyright 2013 the University of Iowa. All rights reserved.

GRADUATION CROWD, THE UNIVERSITY OF IOWA CAMPUS
University Archives, The University of Iowa Libraries. Copyright 2013 the University of Iowa. All rights reserved.

Three days later there was a headline announcing Millie's next step. It read, "Mildred Augustine Society Editor on Clinton Newspaper."[13] She was to begin work for another Iowa newspaper.

But was this truly the end of Millie's educational journey at the University of Iowa?

DID YOU KNOW?

George Gallup would explain his sampling technique in this way: Put seven thousand white beans and three thousand black beans in a barrel and mix them up well. Scoop up one hundred of the beans and you'll get approximately seventy white beans and thirty black beans. The range of error can be determined mathematically. Try this experiment with smaller quantities of beans!

THE FOURTH CLUE

NEXT STEPS

The Case of the Developing Writer

WORKING ON the editorial staff of the society section of the *Clinton Herald* may not have been Millie's ideal position, but it was a job within writing circles. Millie could take what she learned from being a staff member of the *Daily Iowan* and apply it to her new position.

Society sections in today's newspapers usually have short articles and pictures from fundraising events for organizations. During Millie's time with the *Herald*, articles focused on the activities of members of "society," wealthier residents of Clinton. Their birthdays, weddings, and parties were shared with readers.

Millie continued to seek other opportunities while working at the *Herald*. Like many writers today, she may not have earned sufficient income from just one job. Often, writers also teach. Some writers work for newspapers and write books. One of the options Millie explored changed her life.

Millie responded to an advertisement.

By the spring of 1926 the Stratemeyer Syndicate in New York City had been successfully creating children's books for over twenty years. The Syndicate's founder, Edward Stratemeyer, had based his company's practices on his own work experiences.

Edward was born in 1862 in the town of Elizabeth, New Jersey. Like Millie, he aspired from a very young age to become a writer. Like Millie's father, Edward's father was also concerned about whether one could make a living as a writer.

Edward's father told him that he was wasting his time writing. When Edward received his first check—in the amount of seventy-five dollars—for a story he wrote, he took the check directly to his father.

"They paid me that for writing a story," Edward explained.

"Paid you that for writing a story?" Edward's father responded. "Well, you'd better write a lot more of them!"[1]

Edward married Magdalene Van Camp in 1891. Lenna was Edward's nickname for her. Lenna encouraged his love of writing, which Edward pursued through a variety of opportunities.

Edward wrote for several New York-based publishing companies, including Street & Smith. These firms published dime novels, inexpensive paperbacks, with new editions on a weekly basis. They hired writers to create sports and adventure stories and comic and detective novels using an outline that the firm provided to them. Edward was very **prolific** in his writing. He often used one of at least eighteen pseudonyms to write his stories. His skills as a writer were growing.

His family was growing as well. Edward and Lenna's first daughter, Harriet, was born in December 1892, and their second, Edna, arrived in May 1895. With a family to support, Edward needed even more work. He began to explore the developing children's book market. Edward created a story series, the Bound to Win Series, and then wrote several

EDWARD STRATEMEYER IN HIS HOME OFFICE
Manuscripts and Archives Division, The New York Public Library, Astor, Lenox, and
Tilden Foundations

DIME NOVELS & STORY PAPERS

JUST IMAGINE what life would have been like in the early 1900s, when Millie was born. Your home would not have had a television, video games, computers, or even a radio. As was the case in Ladora, Millie's hometown, your community might not even have had a library! What would you have done for reading material before all these other entertainment options became available?

If you liked to read, you could have walked up to the local store and bought a story paper or dime novel. They were inexpensive, ranging from five to fifteen cents per issue. The novels offered complete stories in one issue. Most story papers continued from issue to issue—a serial—with action-packed stories that kept you hooked![2] The story papers and dime novels of yesterday paved the way for series books featuring the Bobbsey Twins, the Hardy Boys, and Nancy Drew—all the way to Harry Potter!

books based on the Revolutionary War, which sold well. With his smart business sense, Edward determined that children enjoyed reading fictional stories based on real events. The Spanish-American War was making the headlines. Newspaper stories shared the first fight between American and Spanish forces at Manila Bay with American readers. On May 1, 1898, Commodore George Dewey of the American forces defeated a Spanish squadron in that great sea battle.

Edward Stratemeyer was ready for a victory of his own. To capitalize on the headlines, he created the Old Glory Series with its first title, *Under Dewey at Manila, or the War Fortunes of a Castaway.* Then, under the name of Arthur M. Winfield, he created the Rover Boys Series for Young Americans. Edward struck gold. Both boys and girls loved reading of the adventures of the three young brothers named Dick, Tom, and Sam.

In 1904 Edward developed a new series featuring two sets of twins. Bert and Nan were twelve years old; Freddie and Flossie were six. Their last name was Bobbsey.

With the success of both series, Edward decided it was time to form his own business, the Stratemeyer Syndicate. He took what he had learned while writing and working for Street & Smith, and hired ghostwriters to follow story outlines. Each outline provided the characters' names and the story's plot for a book in his series. The writers would write under a pseudonym created for each series. That way, any number of writers could write for a series, and readers would not know the difference.

Edward edited the manuscripts himself. He would pay the writer a flat fee, for which the author would agree to give up all his or her rights to the story. The writers could not sell the story otherwise. The individuals writing the stories also agreed to allow the story to be published under a different name, the pseudonym. This name could not be used for anything a writer wrote on his or her own.

To attract new writers, Edward placed advertisements in *The Editor*, a weekly publication intended for authors and writers.

The ad read like this:

THE STRATEMEYER SYNDICATE
315 Fourth Avenue, New York, NY
Stories: "Stories are wanted that can be used in the preparation of the Syndicate's books for boys, books for girls, and rapid-fire detective stories."
Payment: "Rates of payment depend entirely upon the amount of work and the quality."
Edward Stratemeyer is the proprietor.[3]

ON April 17, 1926, Millie sent a letter to the offices of the Stratemeyer Syndicate, inquiring about writing for the Syndicate. Her letter stated her **writing credits,** which included selling twenty-eight short stories in the past two years. Millie also wrote, "I have turned out about six-hundred printed inches of newspaper material for the last year." She closed the letter by offering that she planned to move to New York City in September.[4]

A letter, dated April 21, 1926, from the Stratemeyer Syndicate arrived at Millie's residence on Ninth Avenue in Clinton. Millie must have been nervous as she opened the envelope. The letter stated that the Syndicate did not accept short stories of any kind. It went on to say that all of their stories for children were in book form of up to forty thousand words.

The letter was unsigned, but the typed initials "HOS," for Harriet Otis Smith, Edward Stratemeyer's assistant, appeared at the bottom of the page.

The letter went on to say that if Millie had "anything particularly interesting in the way of regular stories for girls or children which you would like to have me look over in order to get an idea of your style, I shall be pleased to do so if you will send them to this office."[5]

Millie wrote back right away. On May 10, Edward himself replied that he had read her stories and thought he could use her services, assuming they could come to terms.[6]

Meanwhile, writing dreams were temporarily set aside as Millie fulfilled another. She wanted to travel to Europe during the summer of 1926. Her parents refused to let her go alone, so they accompanied her.[7]

In the scrapbook that she created for Millie, her mother noted, "A desire to travel resulted in a trip to Europe." Lillian listed the countries on the itinerary, including England, Holland, Belgium, France, Switzerland, and Italy.[8]

Millie's family still treasures a beautiful, black, sleeveless "flapper" dress and matching purse bought in Paris during their travels. The undated photo of the three of them was likely taken during their trip. Perhaps they were discussing the uncertainty of Millie's future.

MILLIE WITH HER PARENTS, DR. J. L. AND LILLIAN AUGUSTINE,
IN EUROPE
From the private collection of the Mildred Augustine Wirt Benson family

Millie and her parents arrived back in the States on the Cunard Line RMS *Andania II* docking in New York City on Sunday, August 29, 1926. They had set sail from Cherbourg, France, ten days earlier.[9]

While in New York, Millie met with Edward Stratemeyer. He didn't offer any writing opportunities immediately, but she hoped that would change. But the possibility of work wasn't enough to keep Millie in New York as she had planned. Instead, Millie returned to the University of Iowa, seeking her master's degree.

Millie continued to correspond with Edward, sending her new address in Iowa City, 113 E. Court Street. She hoped that he would extend her an invitation to become one of the ghostwriters he was hiring for his expanding series of books for both boys and girls.

She didn't sit around and wait, however. She jumped right back into being actively involved on campus, including rejoining the Seals and working for the *Daily Iowan*.

Millie was soon to be given the opportunity to write about something other than campus activities.

Millie's life was about to change both professionally and personally.

DID YOU KNOW?

Iowa City, home to the University of Iowa, is a very literary city. So much so that you can stroll down Iowa Avenue and see plaques dedicated to the many writers who have studied or lived here. And, of course, there is a plaque for Millie! Perhaps you can go visit and find it!

NEW NAME, NEW CHARACTER, NEW BEGINNING

The Case of the Ghostwriter

"I THOUGHT YOU were on vacation, Ruth!"[1]

So begins the very first children's book Millie wrote for the Stratemeyer Syndicate. *Ruth Fielding and Her Great Scenario* was the twenty-third book in the Ruth Fielding series created in 1913 by Edward Stratemeyer. The story focuses on Ruth, a young orphan taken in by her great-uncle and nurtured by his housekeeper. Ruth's best friend is Helen Cameron. The two girls went to high school together, and then continued on to college. Helen's brother, Tom, is Ruth's fiancé.

Millie, writing under the pseudonym of Alice B. Emerson, shares Ruth's adventures as she is writing a scenario—a screenplay—for a contest with a huge cash prize. The plot involves several action sequences as the script is stolen. Ruth and her friends solve the crime just in time for Ruth to mail off the contest entry.

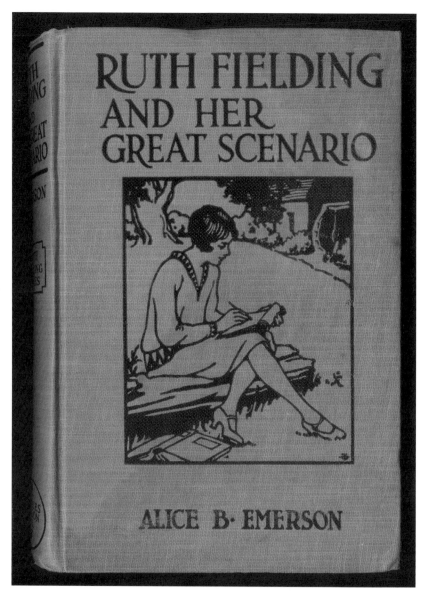

MILLIE'S FIRST WORK FOR THE STRATEMEYER SYNDICATE,
RUTH FIELDING AND HER GREAT SCENARIO, 1927

Ruth Fielding and Her Great Scenario, Alice B. Emerson, Cupples & Leon. Permission
granted from Penguin Group (USA) LLC.

In the end, Ruth wins the contest. The bad guy is punished. And Ruth and Tom manage to work their way through Ruth's concerns about getting married and having a career. Ruth is an independent, strong, young woman who "wanted a career as well as love."[2]

Millie struggled with the story—"it fought me on every page"— because she had difficulties relating to the main character.[3]

Millie submitted the manuscript to Edward Stratemeyer. He replied, "As the story now stands, I think it will prove a fairly good 'Ruth Fielding' yarn, perhaps better than some and not so good as others. But I think you did very well for a first effort."[4]

Millie also made sure to follow Edward's rule in keeping readers loyal to a series. He wanted his writers to reference the previous stories of a series, as well as its future titles. Millie mentions the original Ruth Fielding story, *Ruth Fielding of the Red Mill,* early on in her first book for the Syndicate.[5]

Although Millie stated that she could not relate to the character of Ruth Fielding, the two were similar in a few ways. Ruth, also, was a writer, who sometimes struggled with her craft. "Some days ideas just came—and on other days they would not come."[6]

In her story about Ruth, Millie wrote, "Her writing was destined to be interrupted in an unexpected way."[7]

Little did Millie know that these same words would be true for her own life. For Millie, that unexpected way came in the form of a man by the name of Asa Alvin Wirt.

Asa was a telegraph operator, working for the Associated Press in Iowa City. He took classes at the University of Iowa. Perhaps Millie was impressed with his maturity, as he was nineteen years older. She must have been charmed by his blue eyes and his awareness of current events as they came through on the AP wire.

Her father's influence—a strong work ethic—took hold as Millie managed to balance her work on her master's degree, her relationship with Asa, and her writing. Mr. Stratemeyer gave her the opportunity to write *Ruth Fielding at Cameron Hall,* the next title in the series

MILLIE AND ASA WIRT
From the private collection of the Mildred Augustine Wirt Benson family

ASSOCIATED PRESS & THE TELETYPE

TELEGRAPH OPERATORS had very exciting jobs. They were the first to receive news from around the world and the first to share news from their communities with the rest of the world. Special codes were developed, Morse and Phillips, to transmit the news to the operator who would then translate that message. The invention of the printing telegraphic machine increased the speed of translation and transmission of news significantly, from 50 words per minute to up to 120 words per minute. The type of machine used in the 1920s by the Associated Press was known as the "teletype."[8]

Eventually a new code, wirespeak, was developed and used by the Associated Press staffers. This "language" is a combination of abbreviated, contracted, and misspelled words.[9] You could say wirespeak is the predecessor to texting!

Q: What do you think Sappest means in wirespeak?

A: "Sooner than as soon as possible." You could text that to your friends the next time you want to hang out!

published by Cupples & Leon. Millie wrote the manuscript on a type-writer in the journalism school. Her professors thought she was working on her **thesis**![10]

On Monday, June 6, 1927, Millie was awarded a Master of Arts from the School of Journalism at the university. She was the first person—male or female—to accomplish this feat.[11]

On Sunday, March 4, 1928, Millie and Asa married in Chicago in front of family members and friends. A dinner at the chic Palmer House

Hotel followed the ceremony. The hotel was the perfect romantic setting for a wedding reception. It was also an ideal location for two journalists to get married, for the hotel had a story of its own.

The original Palmer House was a wedding gift from Potter Palmer to his beloved wife, Bertha.[12] (Potter was the owner of the **mercantile** house which came to be known as Marshall Fields.) The hotel burned down thirteen days later during the Great Chicago Fire. Mr. Palmer rebuilt the hotel. Eventually, he built an even bigger hotel on the same site. The new hotel opened the year before Millie and Asa were wed.

The lobby of the hotel was, and is, breathtaking. The ceiling features beautiful panels with scenes from Greek mythology. The winged angels in the lobby were created by Louis Comfort Tiffany, also known for his **Tiffany** lamps.

Millie and Asa were married in one Midwestern city. Their lives together started in another.

The newlyweds moved to Cleveland, Ohio, where Asa's work with the Associated Press took him. Millie's scrapbook tells the story of their early days as husband and wife.

Millie saved a ticket stub from an All Star Boxing match on the evening of April 26, 1928. She held on to programs from shows that were part of the summer theater season in Cleveland. She and Asa would have laughed at the comedy *The Constant Wife* and, perhaps, held hands while they enjoyed a play about the American carnival life, *The Barker*.[13]

Millie continued her daily swimming at the Young Women's Christian Association, the YWCA, and taught swimming lessons at the Brooklyn and Central branches of the Y.

But, despite her marriage to Asa, Millie had every intention of following through with her writing goals and dreams. In the late 1920s married women made up just 25 percent of the female workforce. For every four working women during this time, only one was married.[14]

Millie was ahead of her time.

TIFFANY ANGEL WINGS IN THE PALMER HOUSE HOTEL

Photograph by Bill Huber. © Huberphotography.com

Millie began writing a series under her own name. She also kept communicating with Edward Stratemeyer, informing him of her new wedded status, her address, and her desire to continue to write for him.[15] Edward wrote back to her.

He had Millie in mind for a new series for girls.

DID YOU KNOW?

The chocolate brownie was invented by a chef at the Palmer House Hotel at the request of Mrs. Palmer for something that was cake-like, but smaller, for the lunches of ladies attending the World's Fair in 1893.

THE PALMER HOUSE BROWNIE

The first reference to the "brownie" in America appears in the *Sears Roebuck Catalog* published in Chicago in 1898. The brownie was created in the Palmer House kitchen in the late nineteenth century. The recipe below is the same one used for the brownie served in the Palmer House Hilton today. It remains one of the hotel's most popular confections.

Bertha Palmer's Brownie

Ingredients:
14 oz. semi-sweet chocolate
1 lb. butter
12 oz. granulated sugar
8 oz. flour
4 large whole eggs
12 oz. crushed walnuts
Vanilla extract

Preparation:
Preheat oven to 300 degrees.
Melt chocolate with butter in a double boiler.
Mix dry ingredients into mixing bowl, except walnuts.
Mix chocolate/butter blend with dry ingredients, for four to five minutes.
Add eggs and vanilla.

Pour into a 9 x 12-inch baking pan, sprinkle walnuts on top, press walnuts down slightly into mixture with your hand, and bake at 300° for thirty to forty minutes. You will know when the brownies are done as the edges will start to become a little crispy and the brownies will have risen about one-quarter inch. Note: Even when the brownie is properly baked it will test "gooey" with a toothpick in the middle due to the richness of the mixture.

After removing the pan from the oven, allow the brownies to cool about thirty minutes before spreading a thin layer of the glaze on top with a pastry brush.

Glaze:
1 cup water
1 cup apricot preserves
1 teaspoon unflavored gelatin

Mix together the water, preserves, and unflavored gelatin in a saucepan. Mix thoroughly and bring to a boil for two minutes. SPREAD THE GLAZE MIXTURE ON THE COOLED BROWN-IES WHILE IT IS HOT. *Special Tip:* The brownies are easier to cut if you place them in the freezer for about three to four hours after glazing.[16]

NANCY DREW

The Case of the Young Detective

Nancy Drew grew from the imagination of Edward Stratemeyer, who had created eighteen book series for girls before she arrived on the scene. Nancy had blond hair and blue eyes, with a **roadster** to match. Her father encouraged her adventures as long as she stayed safe.[1] The father, a lawyer, had already lost his wife, and his only child was the apple of his eye.

The idea of Nancy was presented to Millie, who had big dreams as a writer. Even though Millie was new to the Stratemeyer Syndicate fold, she accepted the challenge to write about this young, independent detective.

Mildred Augustine Wirt was now writing as Carolyn Keene, the pseudonym Edward Stratemeyer had chosen for the new Nancy Drew Mystery Stories.

Little did either Edward or Millie realize the impact that this character would have on girls and boys throughout the country. *Throughout the world.*

The Nancy Drew Mystery Stories series was created out of Edward's amazing ability to determine what young readers wanted combined with Millie's desire to establish herself as a writer. She cranked out the original stories within a four- to five-week time frame.

Millie agreed to a flat rate payment of $125 per book, about two months' salary for a newspaper reporter then.[2] She signed a contract similar to the one provided to her for the Ruth Fielding series. She knew that she would not receive royalties from book sales. Millie also agreed that she would not write any other books, outside of those commissioned by the Syndicate, under the pseudonym of Carolyn Keene.

The first three books of the series were to be titled *The Secret of the Old Clock, The Hidden Staircase,* and *The Bungalow Mystery.* New series were often introduced in a collection of three books, released at the same time. The three volumes were known as a "breeder set."

Stratemeyer had negotiated with the publisher, Grosset & Dunlap, a selling price of fifty cents apiece to keep the books affordable for young readers.[3] This decision soon made a big difference in the survival of the series as our country faced the beginnings of the Great Depression.

On October 3, 1929, Edward Stratemeyer sent the outline for *The Secret of the Old Clock* to Millie. Just twenty-six days later the headlines in the *Daily Iowan,* the *Cleveland Plain Dealer,* and the *New York Times* all read the same. The stock market had crashed.

Stocks that had been bought at higher prices began to drop rapidly in value. On Monday, October 28, the value of stocks dropped 13 percent. The next day their value dropped another 12 percent. Tuesday, October 29, 1929, is known as Black Tuesday.

Many people lost a lot of money. Most families couldn't afford anything other than food and clothing—except, perhaps, a popular children's book priced at just fifty cents.

Fortunately for all of us, Nancy Drew survived this first of many challenges.

Young readers were ready to read about a new, independent character. The Nineteenth Amendment to the United States Constitution, guaranteeing the right for all women to vote, had been **ratified** in August 1920. Women were beginning to enjoy more freedom than ever before, and books for young readers were beginning to reflect this. Ninety-four new series featuring young, strong, female **protagonists** were published between 1910 and 1930.[4]

Nancy Drew's time had come. The plot of *The Secret of the Old Clock* involved the missing will of a character, Josiah Crowley, that had been stashed secretly by members of the wealthy and cruel Topham family.

Millie took the outline and ran with it, creating the essence of Nancy, the feisty heroine the world has grown to love.

Millie drew upon her childhood imagination to flesh out the outline she had received from Stratemeyer. Nancy was the type of girl that everyone wanted to be. She had no concerns about money, no interest in boys (at first, anyway), and a dear friend named Helen. She had a housekeeper and a very understanding and doting father, Carson Drew. Nancy wasn't afraid to dig in and get the job done, learning from her father. "I've often heard Father say that no real mystery is solved without a lot of hard work—and I'm ready to believe it!"[5]

Whether she was fixing her own flat tire, or outsmarting the bad guys who had locked her into a closet, Nancy wasn't rescued by anyone. She figured out how to get out of a jam on her own. She was very athletic, and kept calm under most circumstances.

That winter of 1929 Millie wrote the first of the new Nancy Drew Mystery Stories. As Asa went off to work, Millie remained at their home on Roycroft Avenue in Lakewood, writing about the adventures of the young detective.

After Millie finished the first story, she sent it to Edward. He responded to her as an editor would respond to a new writer. Edward told her what he didn't like in the manuscript. "I thought the first half of the story was a bit slow and that the characters were not sufficiently introduced." He also addressed what he felt was strong in her writing. "But as soon as Nancy gets to New Moon Lake the story picks up very well indeed and the last eight chapters are particularly strong."[6]

Edward, apparently, was also a little concerned with her characterization of the courageous, independent young detective who dared to question her elders when the occasion called for it.

"Girls' books and boys' books in his mind followed a certain pattern and if you broke that pattern, it bothered him. He didn't think that I created the character of Nancy in a way that he anticipated," Millie offered in an interview just several years before she died. "He was fairly liberal and he submitted it as I wrote it to the publisher. The publisher was very enthusiastic right from the start, so it went forward just as I wrote it."[7]

And forward it went.

Edward sent a letter dated December 3, 1929, inquiring as to whether the outline for the second book, *The Hidden Staircase,* appealed to Millie and whether she would be able to complete it in time for spring publication, as the publishers were "quite anxious to get the three books just as soon as possible."[8]

Millie may have been pressed for time in writing the first three volumes, but Edward was facing a much more challenging crisis.

He was very sick.

Edward Stratemeyer developed a **thrombosis** of the leg—a blood clot—in February 1930. The clot cleared up, but he suffered two heart attacks and ultimately developed pneumonia.[9]

Edward was sick at his home in New Jersey most of that winter, with his assistant, Harriet Otis Smith, taking care of business back at his offices in New York City. It was Miss Smith who read Millie's work on the third book of the series, *The Bungalow Mystery.* Miss Smith helped, with Edward's guidance, to get the edited Nancy Drew stories to the publisher in time.[10]

THE HIDDEN STAIRCASE, THE SECOND TITLE IN THE NANCY
DREW MYSTERY STORIES SERIES, 1930

The Hidden Staircase, Carolyn Keene, Grosset & Dunlap. Permission granted by Penguin
Group (USA) LLC.

THE BUNGALOW MYSTERY COMPLETED THE NANCY DREW
BREEDER SET RELEASED IN 1930

The Bungalow Mystery, Carolyn Keene, Grosset & Dunlap. Permission granted by Penguin
Group (USA) LLC.

NANCY DREW: HER FANS
AND HER LEGACY

EDWARD STRATEMEYER created an icon in Nancy Drew. Millie established her identity and wrote of Nancy's adventures through twenty-three of the original thirty Nancy Drew Mystery Stories. Harriet Stratemeyer Adams, along with future ghostwriters, carried Nancy's torch even beyond each of their own lives. Several movies and a television series were based on her character. Nancy is alive and well today, through a new series and a variety of computer and video games.

Nancy's independent spirit, sense of adventure, and ability to solve her own problems, as well as others' mysteries, touched many readers' lives over the years. Women, particularly, found Nancy Drew to be an inspiration, as she came on the scene when opportunities for women were limited. Nancy, although fictitious, proved that young women could do anything they set their minds to.

Millie, Harriet Stratemeyer Adams, and Harriet's sister, Edna, proved this as well with their efforts not only in keeping the spirit of Nancy alive, but by continuing to do so, through a Great Depression, the loss of Edward, and, even, the legal challenges that came many years later.

Young readers were able to purchase their copies of the first Nancy Drew mysteries on Monday, April 28, 1930. The initial three books were a success from the beginning. The mysteries sold just shy of 43,000 copies in 1930 at a time when many people were out of work, farmers couldn't afford to harvest their crops, and families stood in line at soup kitchens.[11]

By then, Millie was already working on the next story for Edward. He sent her the outline for *The Mystery at Lilac Inn* in late April. Millie responded that she would have the manuscript in his hands in the time frame he requested. It would be their last correspondence.[12]

On Saturday, May 10, just twelve days after the series' release, Edward Stratemeyer died at his home. The single most influential figure in the field of twentieth-century juvenile series books was gone.[13]

He left behind his wife, Lenna, who had been ill for many years, two daughters, and four grandchildren. Edward also left behind a business that very few knew much about, much less how to operate. His family was devastated and the publishing industry was nervous about what would happen to the many series the Syndicate had been producing. The ghostwriters who had written for Edward were left wondering what the future held.

One of them was Millie.

Appropriately, Edward Stratemeyer's **epitaph** on his gravestone reads, "THE FINAL CHAPTER CLOSES, LEAVING IN YOUNG HEARTS THE MEMORY OF FINE IDEALS."

Had the chapter closed on the Stratemeyer Syndicate? Were Nancy Drew's adventures over not long after they started? What was to become of her? What about Millie? What would happen with the character and the writer now that Edward Stratemeyer was gone?

DID YOU KNOW?

Nancy Drew's girlfriends George Fayne and Bess Marvin did not appear in the Nancy Drew Mystery Stories until *The Secret at Shadow Ranch*.[14] Nancy's boyfriend, Ned Nickerson, first appeared in *The Clue in the Diary*.[15]

DIFFERENT CHARACTERS/ SIMILAR LIVES

The Case of the Prolific Writer

EDWARD STRATEMEYER did not have sons to entrust his business to upon his death. He had two daughters, Harriet and Edna. Edward had begun creating series for girls to read that featured independent and strong women. But in real life, he was doing so in an era when many, including Edward, believed women belonged in the home.

At the time of their father's death, Harriet was a homemaker with four children. Edna remained at their family home, helping both her mother and father during their illnesses. The daughters knew little of the business. The Depression had just begun, and although President Hoover stated on May 1, 1930, that the worst was over, this was not the case.[1] It would be difficult to sell the business based on the state of the country's economy.

Harriet and Edna worked together, along with their father's long-time assistant, Harriet Otis Smith, to save the Stratemeyer Syndicate. They moved the offices from New York City to New Jersey, closer to their homes. Edna worked on the accounting side of the business, her sister Harriet contacted publishers, and Harriet Otis Smith contacted ghostwriters.

One of those writers was none other than Millie.

Millie was asked to write the next Nancy Drew mystery! Millie wrote to Miss Smith that she was happy to write the fifth book. Millie let Harriet know that if she sent the outline right away, she could write the book before a planned vacation.[2]

Millie needed a vacation. She was writing both the Ruth Fielding Series books and the latest Nancy Drew Mystery Stories. Millie had also begun a new series on her own, based on a historical event that occurred near her new home in Cleveland.

On August 18, 1929, twenty female pilots competed in the first Air Derby—a flying race—that began in Santa Monica, California. For nine days they flew solo across the country. They made their way to the ultimate destination of the Cleveland Municipal Airport, just twenty minutes away from Millie. Among the pilots were Amelia Earhart and the eventual winner, Louise Thaden.

One of the younger pilots lost her maps while in **turbulence** over Arizona. She landed in a field to get her bearings. Her red plane attracted the attention of the grazing bulls in the field, as well as that of the farmer's wife. Neither the cows nor the wife were very pleased with the disturbance.

This pretty **aviatrix** wore fancy ribbons in her hair and captured the hearts of America. She was the first woman to attempt to cross the Atlantic in 1927.[3]

Her name was Ruth Elder.[4]

Millie had a new heroine of her own. And she discovered a new passion: aviation.

AVIATRIX RUTH ELDER SERVED AS INSPIRATION FOR THE RUTH
DARROW FLYING STORIES

Smithsonian Institution per Henry Holden

Millie created the *Ruth Darrow Flying Stories*, writing the four volumes under her own name. Plucked right from the headlines that happened in her backyard, the first story involves a new airplane race for women, created by Colonel Darrow, Ruth's father. Colonel Darrow hopes to encourage more women to become interested in flying, so he donates a special silver trophy as the prize. Ruth, along with her friend Jean, has taken flying lessons and obtained her pilot's license. It is her hope to keep the trophy in the family, so she signs up for the race. The trophy disappears and Ruth's plane has mechanical difficulties.

Rest assured that the mystery is solved, Ruth's plane is fixed, and the derby takes place. Any guesses as to who wins the coveted silver trophy?

Ruth Darrow and Nancy Drew had similar qualities and lifestyles. Both of their mothers were deceased. They had wonderful relationships with their fathers. They both had a special friend to confide in. They were fiercely independent and confident. They were sixteen, athletic, attractive, and heroic.

The storyline for every book in both the Nancy Drew Mystery Stories and the Ruth Darrow Flying Stories involved a mystery with a happy ending. Each book had twenty-five chapters and just over two hundred pages.

Millie was learning from the Stratemeyer Syndicate "formula" and outlines and applying them to her own writing.

She was finding her voice as a writer for the juvenile market.

And what a voice it was.

Millie wrote over 130 children's books during her long career. Over half of them were written and published between 1927 and 1941.

The Syndicate contracted with Millie to write for the Dana Girls Mystery Stories. Millie also continued to write for the Nancy Drew Mystery Stories, and about Kay Tracey's adventures in *The Six Fingered Glove Mystery* and *The Green Cameo Mystery*.

Millie also wrote several series about young female sleuths that were not published by the Stratemeyer Syndicate.

THE FIRST RUTH DARROW BOOK, *RUTH DARROW IN THE AIR DERBY,* 1930

Ruth Darrow in the Air Derby, Mildred A. Wirt, Barse & Co. Permission granted from Penguin Group (USA) LLC.

The Penny Nichols Mystery Series, written under the pseudonym Joan Clark, featured a bold fifteen-year-old girl whose widowed father ran a detective agency.[5]

Young readers snuggled in with another new character, Margaret "Peggy" Palmer, in *The Clue at Crooked Lane,* one of the Mildred A. Wirt Mystery Stories published by Cupples & Leon. Peggy was being raised by her father, following the death many years ago of her mother, and had a best friend, Rebecca.

In 1939 Millie introduced the world to Penny Parker. Entirely Millie's creation, "Penny Parker," Millie stated, "was a better Nancy Drew than Nancy Drew was."[6] Penny was bolder and even more independent than Nancy. Her widowed father was an editor of a newspaper. Naturally, Penny was a reporter who had a penchant for discovering and solving mysteries. She had just one close friend, Louise, a rather quiet sidekick. Penny had "personality plus" and was not afraid to speak her mind. She was Millie's favorite fictional heroine.

While readers were introduced to these new young characters, Millie announced another one of her very own to the Stratemeyer sisters.

On January 10, 1937, Millie wrote to Edna.

"You and Mrs. Adams may be interested to know that early in November I gave birth to a blue-eyed, red-headed, baby girl. My work this past year was somewhat difficult, but at present I am in excellent health, thoroughly enjoying both my writing and the new baby."[7]

Edna wrote back. "It is a mystery to us, à la Kay Tracey, how you were able to manage so well with your writing and your household last year. We do congratulate you upon the birth of a daughter and should like to hear her ***nom de plume***. That wisp of red hair sounds most intriguing."[8]

Asa and Millie named their daughter Margaret, or Peggy for short. Apparently Millie could keep a secret. Very soon she would have another one that she kept to herself for some time. This one would be difficult to bear.

BABY PEGGY WIRT
Mildred Wirt Benson Papers, Iowa Women's Archives, The University of Iowa Libraries.

FIRST FEMALE FLYERS AND
THE POWDER PUFF DERBY

WOMEN ACCOMPLISHED many "firsts" in the field of aviation in the early 1900s. Harriet Quimby was the first licensed aviatrix in 1911 and Bessie Coleman became the first internationally licensed African American pilot, male or female, in 1921.[9]

The women who strapped on their flying helmets and took to the skies in the all-female cross-country air race from Santa Monica, California, to Cleveland, Ohio, on August 18, 1929, were the first to do so. Ever.

As the pilots took off, Will Rogers, a humorist, commented, "It looks like a Powder Puff Derby to me." His comment was not intended to be sexist, as he had the utmost respect for the women. The name stuck.[10]

The women were competing not only for the title of champion, but also for a shot at a total of twenty-five thousand dollars in prize money. The race distance from Jim and Clema Granger's aviation operation, Clover Field, in Santa Monica, to the municipal airport in Cleveland was roughly 2,700 miles. The race included multiple stops, with each community along the way trying to outdo the other in terms of hospitality. The female pilots would have preferred to be left alone to check the weather, their maps, their gear, and their planes.

The newspaper journalists felt otherwise. These women were pioneers in their field, and Americans wanted to know about their exciting endeavors. Perhaps Millie was one of those watching as the pilots flew, one by one, into the Cleveland airfield on Monday, August 26, 1929.

Louise Thaden won the race, with a total of twenty hours, nineteen minutes, and four seconds of actual flying time over the course of nine days. After barreling over the finish line at 170 mph, she graciously accepted the prize money and accolades, stating, "I'm sorry we all couldn't come in first, because they all deserve it as much as I. They're all great flyers."[11]

DID YOU KNOW?

Ruth Elder, Amelia Earhart, Louise Thaden, and ninety-six other female pilots formed an organization, The Ninety-Nines, Inc., on November 2, 1929, in a hangar at Curtiss Field in Long Island, New York. Of the 117 licensed female pilots in the country at the time, 99 showed up to start the organization to promote advancement in aviation. Today the membership involves female professional pilots, pilots who teach others to fly, and women who simply love to fly.

Just four years earlier, a future pilot was born. Geraldine "Jerrie" Fredritz Mock was born in 1925. Jerrie's record-setting solo flight around the world is the subject of a forthcoming book in the Biographies for Young Readers Series.

SAD LOSS & NEW BEGINNING

The Case of the Budding Journalist

MILLIE'S PUBLISHING record tells a story.

In 1940 Millie had twelve books published. In 1941 she had just five.

Five books published in a single year is a dream for any writer. But for Millie to have gone from having twelve books published one year to fewer than half that number the following year tells us something. From 1941 through 1960, the year her last children's book was published, Millie never had more than five books published in any given year.

What happened?

We need to get out our magnifying glasses and look a little deeper into Millie's personal life to solve this mystery.

ASA AND PEGGY
From the private collection of the Mildred Augustine Wirt Benson family

The year 1940 offered much change and challenge for the Wirt family. The Associated Press had transferred Asa to the Toledo office several years before. The family moved into their home, Millie's last home, on Middlesex Drive that year. Then Asa became ill.

Asa suffered a cerebral hemorrhage—a stroke—that took its toll on him. In January 1941 Millie wrote to Edna Stratemeyer Squier about her husband's health. (Edna had married in 1937.) She shared that, although Asa's condition was serious, he was recovering. Sadly, the recovery did not last long.[1]

By July 1941 Asa took a leave of absence from the Associated Press due to the effects of the stroke. Although he worked occasionally after that point, he continued to suffer from a series of other strokes that left him bedridden.

Millie wrote to Harriet Stratemeyer Adams in May of 1942 that Asa was "much improved in health, which in turn has made my work easier."[2] Asa may have had a slight, temporary improvement, but Millie chose to keep the severity of his condition to herself. She was very private and secretive about her husband's health. By 1943 Asa's days as a teletype operator were over.[3]

In July 1944 Millie wrote to Harriet that she had taken a new position with the Toledo Community Chest as a publicity writer. She added that Asa was in very poor health, having suffered five strokes by that point. And, she shared, "I feel it wise to take on salary work during this period when women are so much in demand."[4]

This was a difficult time for the United States. Many men were serving in World War II, leaving their jobs temporarily. Women, like Millie, stepped up to fill roles that had been traditionally held by men.

As a result of the shortage of male employees, Millie landed a job with the *Toledo Times* as a city hall "**beat**" reporter in the fall of 1944. Millie was transitioning from children's book writer to journalist.

As Asa was often bedridden during his illness, Millie would type away on her old Underwood typewriter beside his bed. Millie's mother,

MILLIE AND PEGGY SLEDDING

Lillian, came to stay with the family to help with Peggy and Asa while Millie headed out to her *Times* assignments.[5]

It was a hard time for the whole family. Peggy was quite close to her grandmother. Although family pictures reflect happy times between Millie and her daughter, her relationship with Peggy was challenging.

Displayed within Millie's scrapbook of newspaper articles from this time are pieces on Toledo city government issues. As a "cub," or new, reporter, Millie was not yet getting credit for her many articles. But her journalism training from the University of Iowa was reflected in her work. The "who, what, when, where, and how" requirements for a story were covered in each article.

Millie was developing her style, while paying her dues as the new reporter. Millie was learning what it meant to "have a **lead**," an angle of how a story was to be pursued and presented. And pursue she did.

Years later she spoke of how she wanted to interview a county commissioner about a topic. His secretary had told her that the commissioner was in a meeting, but Millie knew he did not want to talk to her. She was not going to give up. She sat outside his office all day waiting for him to come out. At the end of the day, she learned that he had snuck out of the window to avoid her![6]

Eventually her hard work and diligence paid off.

By March of 1945 Millie's **byline** was appearing in the *Times* for various articles. Her interest in aviation, particularly concerning female pilots, came through in various assignments. These included an interview with Alice Krueger, who taught many male pilots during World War II how to fly.[7]

Throughout the war, Millie wrote about the effects of wartime at home. Butter and milk prices had skyrocketed and flour was available only in limited quantities, causing concern about lines to buy bread. Can you imagine having to wait in line to buy bread?

Millie wrote about "war brides," women who had arrived from other countries and married in Toledo, but were now homesick.

After she had filed her stories, Millie went back home to her young daughter, her sick husband, and her mother. Then she sat at her typewriter and began work on her next children's book.

Millie continued to write for the Stratemeyer Syndicate. However, her correspondence with Harriet Adams reflects her frustration with the increasing amount of rewriting occurring on the Nancy Drew stories. "One of the reasons, I feel, is that the outline is too full, with many big scenes in each chapter."[8]

Harriet had become increasingly demanding and critical of Millie's writing.

Both women were going through personal challenges. Millie's husband was very sick, and Harriet was at odds with her sister, Edna, as to how to resolve the issue of the toll Millie's personal life was taking on her writing. Harriet felt it was time to step away from their relationship with Millie.

WAR BRIDES

IT IS estimated that, between 1942 and 1952, over one million American soldiers married women from over fifty different countries. Young women from around the world fell in love with the young, strong, handsome soldiers who came bearing food, chocolates, nylon stockings (which were very difficult to come by during the war), and big smiles. The women left their homes, families, and former lives behind in their native countries—all in the name of love. Even though military regulations discouraged these marriages, young soldiers fell in love a million times over and proposed to their foreign girlfriends.

For the time being, Harriet and Edna set aside their disagreement, and Millie was sent an outline for *The Ghost of Blackwood Hall*.

The day she received the outline, May 26, 1947, Asa died.[9] Millie was very sad. Yet, because Asa had been sick for so long, his death lifted the burden of his care from her.

Her letter to Harriet, less than a month later, reflects her long ordeal, and her intent to move forward. "As for myself, we have had so much trouble from the health standpoint these last seven years that I am quite toughened to meeting it head-on. All one can do, in the last analysis, is just carry on."[10]

In true Millie fashion, she dug back into her writing, for the *Times*, for the Syndicate, and for her own books.

Millie had a brief falling out with Harriet after *The Ghost of Blackwood Hall*. For a few years, she did not write any books for the Stratemeyer Syndicate. Instead, she wrote a number of books under her own

MILLIE WITH THE "LOVE OF HER LIFE," GEORGE BENSON
From the private collection of the Mildred Augustine Wirt Benson family

name, including two new series—the Brownie Scout Series and Dan Carter Cub Scout Series.

And she began a new life with a new husband.

Millie wrote a letter to Harriet, dated July 17, 1951, concerning Millie's attempts to coordinate a visit to the Stratemeyer Syndicate offices in New Jersey. Millie shared, "I remarried a little more than a year ago, my husband being George Benson, editorial writer and associate editor of the *Times* where I am still employed as court-house reporter."[11]

George was described as the "love of her life" by family members.[12]

Being married once again provided financial security to Millie. She could have chosen to stop writing and working, but she did not. However, one choice was made for her. The Stratemeyer Syndicate was changing the policies for writing its series. Millie, along with the other ghostwriters, would no longer be contributing to any series. Harriet

A FORMAL PORTRAIT OF MILLIE AND GEORGE BENSON

Mildred Wirt Benson Papers, Iowa Women's Archives, The University of Iowa Libraries.

Adams and other staff members were going to write the books. But Millie was never officially told of the new policy.[13]

The last book of the Nancy Drew Mystery Stories that Millie wrote for the Stratemeyer Syndicate was *The Clue of the Velvet Mask*, published in 1953. The last book that Millie ever wrote for the Syndicate, a Dana Girls Mystery, *Mystery at the Crossroads*, was published the following year.

One era had come to a close for Millie.

Another was about to begin.

DID YOU KNOW?

"Rosie the Riveter" was a character created to urge women to join the workforce during World War ll, particularly to work in factories manufacturing planes, tanks, and other warfare machines. Many men in the United States were off to war and women were needed to fill their jobs. "Rosie" encouraged women to take on roles they had never tried, from streetcar conductors to aerodynamic engineers, all in the name of patriotic duty. The character has been portrayed in a variety of media, and has grown into a symbol of women's independence and rights.

THE NINTH CLUE

TAKE OFF!

The Case of the Flying Reporter

IN 1965 Millie was writing in a different kind of book. Her words were short and concise.

> 9/18/65. Toledo. Local. PA 22. 5721Z. LCY.108.30. **Familiarization** Flight.

The entries are from Millie's pilot logbook. They are a record of her training and, eventually, of her travels. The information includes the date; where she was flying from; where she was flying to; the make, model, and certificate information on her plane; the engine size; its horsepower; and the amount of time flying. In this case, Millie left from and returned to the Toledo area airport, flying dual, with a flight instructor, for thirty minutes.[1]

Yes, Millie was learning how to fly.

But wait a minute. This part of our story takes place in 1965.

When we last left Millie, she was newly married to *Toledo Times* associate editor and writer George Benson. She was balancing her time as a reporter, wife, and mother in the early 1950s.

What happened in between?

Just as Millie's story moved forward quickly, so, too, did Millie, after once again suffering a great loss.

She and George were equals in many ways. They both loved to write. They enjoyed golfing at Heather Downs Country Club, entertaining at the prestigious Toledo Club, and traveling together.

George loved to cook, and he was a good stepfather to Peggy. He brought laughter back into their lives.

He cherished the English language and enjoyed using big words in his editorials. Like Millie, he had been a writer from an early age. He began working as a telegraph editor for the *Grand Forks (ND) Herald* just weeks after he had graduated from high school. Ten years later, he became managing editor of the *Herald*.[2]

From 1930 to 1948 George worked as a writer in a variety of jobs. He was the head of the *Minneapolis Journal's* Washington, D.C., bureau. He then became a **freelance writer**.

George and his first wife moved to Toledo in 1948, but she died shortly afterwards.

Then he met Millie and they began writing a new life together.

Millie continued to write for the *Toledo Times*, the morning paper published by the *Toledo Blade*, covering city hall and, then, writing business stories. She began to write **feature** stories for the *Blade*. At the same time, she raised Peggy as best as she could and enjoyed life with George.

Until the ending to their fairy tale came too soon.

In 1959 George died suddenly of a stroke the day that he and Millie intended to leave on a vacation.

Once again Millie faced the death of her husband. Once again Millie picked herself up and did the best that she could with life's circumstances.

Peggy was a young woman by this time, and Millie was on her own. She would remain so the rest of her life. But she was certainly not lonely.

Millie was fifty-four years old when George died. At an age when many women might consider slowing down, Millie did just the opposite.

As they might say in flight circles, she picked up groundspeed.

Millie looked back to her earliest chapters to write about her own final ones.

WHEN she was a young schoolgirl, a barnstorming pilot—one who flew across the country selling airplane rides—came into Ladora, flying in over the town in his Jenny airplane. Millie scraped together her life savings, all fifteen dollars, and ran off to the takeoff site. She gave her fee to the pilot. She strapped on a helmet and buckled herself into the open cockpit.

The pilot soared the plane up, up, and just over a barn. Millie was so amazed by the skies around her, she didn't discover the sights below until the pilot looked back at her and pointed down. By the time Millie saw her world from up above, it was nearly time to land. She was hooked. Her father learned of her first flight after she had already landed. When Millie begged for another flight, he refused. "You nearly hit that barn," he said. "You're lucky to be alive."[3]

The itch to fly was further fueled by living so close to the Cleveland Municipal Airport, and then by creating the *Ruth Darrow Flying Series*.

Millie's mother Lillian's statement—written so many years before in her memory book, "A desire to travel resulted . . ."—proved true once more. Millie never gave up on this passion either.

New Treasure Found in Lost City of Mayas was the title of a story Millie wrote for the *Toledo Blade* in June 1960. She had discovered a way to put all of her interests together and get paid to write about them. Millie had added another newfound passion to her **repertoire**. She fell in love with the mystery of ancient archeology.

MILDRED WIRT BENSON INTERVIEWING PILOT MARY GAFFANEY, READING, PENNSYLVANIA, 1972

Toledo Blade/Jack Ackerman, photographer, © *The Blade*

Nancy Drew, the sleuth, and Penny Parker, the reporter, had come together.

Millie continued to travel and write about Central America on dozens of trips, traveling by herself and hiring **bush pilots** to take her into the jungles to visit and write about the Mayan ruins.

After having these exciting adventures while flying with a bush pilot, Millie's interest in exploring the skies on her own intensified.

"I was looking for a feature and they had a newspaper ad for five dollars, for which you could have a familiarizing lesson in an airplane. So I went out and took it and wrote a story about it and I liked it so well I went back and it was the most expensive five-dollar coupon I ever had in my life," Millie shared in an interview.[4]

Millie wrote a column, *Happy Landings*, which appeared every other Sunday in the *Blade*. According to a promotional ad from 1969, readers could learn about "flying techniques, piloting practices, interesting places to fly, and much more."

Millie's stories for the *Blade* were as diverse as she was. Her ever-curious mind, combined with her journalistic instincts, made her pose questions that other reporters might not.

Nancy Hawkins, a librarian with the *Blade* and a longtime friend and confidant of Millie's recalled a typical conversation with Millie.

> She'd say, "I'm looking for a story. Do you know anybody?"
>
> I'd reply, "Well, there's this guy who collects thousands of clocks."
>
> Millie would say, "Well, after you say he's got a bunch of clocks, now what?"

Millie was always looking for her lead while investigating any potential articles.

"I will always remember Millie as being a storyteller. Whether through the page, or through her voice, Millie was a storyteller," Nancy recalled.

And how she shared stories! In 1990 she created a weekly column, *On the Go*. Through this new outlet, Millie wrote about her life growing up in Iowa, her fondness for golf, and her continued fascination with aviation. And she left her readers wanting more.

Millie had a **penchant** for encouraging others to share in her passions, and would often reference the resources her readers would need in order to enjoy them as well. In April of 1990, Millie's article with the headline, "For adventure, fly up, up, and away in a beautiful balloon!" told about the pleasures of hot air ballooning.

"Ballooning," she wrote, "is not as safe for a senior as the old rocking chair, but it does offer a unique excitement. So for those able-bodied and eager, why not go for it!"

MILDRED WIRT BENSON IN THE PILOT SEAT
Toledo Blade Historical File, © *The Blade*

Go for it she did. The previous September, at eighty-four years of age, she had taken her first balloon flight with a group of retired aircraft pilots in Albuquerque, New Mexico.

Millie had many flight expeditions throughout her career. But one she would have liked to experience just wasn't meant to be.

"Mildred Benson . . . has demonstrated a high level of professionalism and an expertise in aviation surpassing that of any reporter I've known. She is capable of reporting and writing on high-flying topics in a down-to-earth manner, in language easily understood by those of us who are more tied to the ground."

These words were written by her editor at the *Blade* for a very special application Millie was filling out.[5]

The application was for the National Aeronautics and Space Administration (NASA) journalist-in-space program. Millie wanted to go to outer space!

TAKING FLIGHT:
PILOT CERTIFICATES

A PILOT CERTIFICATE for flying is much like a driver's license for driving. The certificate states the privilege, or skill, level a pilot has achieved—student, sport, recreational, private, commercial, or airline transport pilot. It gives the category, or categories, of aircraft a pilot can operate—airplane, rotorcraft, glider, lighter-than-air, powered lift, powered parachute, or weight-shift-control—and the class within any category. For example, a pilot trained to fly an airplane may have mastered one or more of four classes: single-engine land, single-engine sea, multi-engine land, and multi-engine sea. A rotorcraft pilot may be trained to fly a gyroplane, a helicopter, or both. Certain types of aircraft—larger planes or ones powered by turbojets—may also require a type rating.

The certificate then specifies any limitations and special skills a pilot may have, and whether he or she is visual flight rated (able to navigate only by what he or she sees), or instrument rated (able to navigate using the instrument panel to guide him or her).[6]

By looking at a certificate, we can learn what type, or types, of aircraft a pilot can fly (category and class), and how skilled a pilot is in flying that aircraft (privilege levels and ratings).

Millie received her pilot certificate in the following airplane categories: private pilot single-engine land, private pilot single-engine sea, commercial pilot single-engine land, and commercial pilot single-engine sea. She was instrument rated in all four categories.[7]

In her essay Millie wrote, "From past years as a springboard high diver, the exhilarating sensation of aerial free movement is, for me, a familiar one. How would it compare to weightlessness in space? Hopefully, if I could learn the answer, I might be able to impart to others the joy of winging unafraid into the unknown."

Her essay application is dated January 5, 1986. On January 28, the space shuttle *Challenger* exploded. Teacher-in-space Sharon Christa McAuliffe and six other astronauts perished as an O-ring seal in the shuttle's right booster engine failed. The spaceship exploded just seventy-three seconds into flight. The entire country mourned the loss of the seven crew members.

The journalist-in-space program was grounded before it ever took off.

Millie would not get her chance to explore this last frontier. However, she was about to be sent spiraling into a new realm for her.

The spotlight.

DID YOU KNOW?

Orville and Wilbur Wright, brothers who lived in Dayton, successfully completed the first sustained, heavier-than-air flight in their airplane at Kitty Hawk, North Carolina, on December 17, 1903, nearly two years before Millie was born. In 1969, just two years after Millie got her pilot's license, the United States landed the first manned mission on the moon. In 2002, the year Millie died, the National Aeronautics and Space Administration (NASA) conducted four shuttle missions to the International Space Station.

NANCY DREW CONFERENCE, RECOGNITION & LEGACY

The Case of a Storied Life

MILLIE WALKED out of the courtroom in 1980 likely feeling a sense of righteousness. The world finally knew who the original writer of the Nancy Drew books was. Or did we?

Let's just say that Millie's phone wasn't ringing off the hook after the trial. Even after court documents confirmed Millie's role as the first ghostwriter of the Nancy Drew Mystery Stories, no one seemed to care.

It wasn't until some sleuthing years later by a staff member at the University of Iowa that Millie came to be honored for her significant role in the series.

The journalism school secretary, Susan Redfern, came across Millie's records in the **alumni** files. A lot of research into Millie's accomplishments was conducted. A successful campaign to promote

Millie as a candidate for the university's School of Journalism and Mass Communication Hall of Fame followed. Soon other staff members realized they were onto something, and someone.

Within the files were correspondence between Millie and the university from 1953. Millie had submitted a listing of the books that she had written over the years, including her twenty-three titles of the original thirty Nancy Drew books.

Carolyn Stewart Dyer, a journalism professor, led an organizing committee that intended to explore the Nancy Drew series and honor native Iowan Millie. The organizers also were curious as to how the character of Nancy Drew had affected readers in their own personal lives.[1]

THE small, elderly woman, her back hunched with age, slid into the seat of honor at the **press conference**. She wore a bright turquoise jacket with shiny black and silver buttons. Her hair was in a bit of a curly disarray, but her hands were manicured perfectly. She looked as if this were a big deal for her. It was. Cameras flashed. She winced. She smiled. She sat down in front of the microphone.

"I would, just as a personal favor, ask you to not use my age. I know some of you will probably do it anyway, so, I'm 130 today. So if you are going to violate it, put it in accurately," she said. The reporters laughed, and went on with their questions.[2]

Such was the scene from the Nancy Drew Conference staged at the University of Iowa in April 1993. The subject of the reporters' interest was none other than Mildred Augustine Wirt Benson. For the record, as she liked to say, she was really *just* eighty-seven years old, and still going strong.

The University of Iowa was filled with fans of Nancy Drew for three days that April. Stories could be heard from readers about what a difference Nancy had made in their lives. Professors and historians talked about the ways the character had influenced society. Young children, the next generation of Nancy Drew fans, read, played games, and tried their hand at writing their own mysteries.

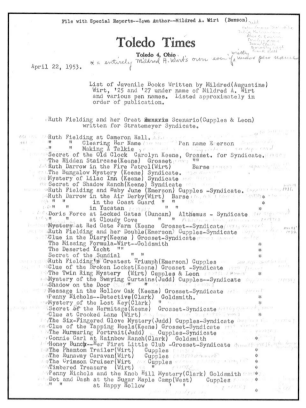

A LIST OF THE JUVENILE BOOKS WRITTEN BY MILDRED WIRT
BENSON AND PUBLISHED UNDER HER NAME AND VARIOUS PEN
NAMES AS COMPILED BY THE *TOLEDO TIMES*

Mildred Wirt Benson Papers, Iowa Women's Archives, The University of Iowa Libraries.
Copyright 2013 the University of Iowa. All rights reserved.

Over five hundred people attended the program. They listened intently to presentations about the history of the Stratemeyer Syndicate. The 1939 film, *Nancy Drew and the Hidden Staircase,* was shown. Young winners of a writing contest read their essays.

At the heart of it all, and in the hearts of many, was Millie.

"I never anticipated any success. I mean, I don't think anyone anticipated the success that Nancy Drew had had. But I did know I was

Toledo Times
Toledo 4, Ohio

page 2   ☆ = entirely Mildred A. Wirt's own even if written under pen name

Dot and Dash in the North Woods(West) Cupples   ☆
Through the Moongate Door (Wirt)   Cupples   ☆
Message in the Sand Dunes(Judd) Cupples
Mystery of the Locked Room   Keene) Grosset-Syndicate   ☆
Wooden Shoe Mystery(Wirt)   Cupples
The Haunted Bridge(Keene)   Grosset-Syndicate
Beneath the Crimson Brier Bush(Judd) Cupples-Syndicate
The Whispering Statue (Wirt)(Keene) Grosset-Syndicate
Secret of the Windmill(Judd) Cupples-Syndicate
Honey Bunch-Her First Little Treasure-Grosset-Syndicate
The Shadow Stone(Wirt)   Cupples   ☆
Circle of Footsteps(Keene) Grosset-Syndicate   ☆
Secret of the Black Imp(Wirt)   Goldsmith
Mystery of the Ivory Charm(Judd) Cupples-Syndicate
Courageous Wings(Wirt)   Penn   ☆
Green Cameo Mystery(Judd) Cupples -Syndicate
Hollow Wall Mystery(Wirt) Cupples   ☆
Honey Bunch-Her First Trip in a Trailer(Grosset-Syndicate
Tale of the Witch Doll (Wirt) Cupples   ☆
The Vanishing Houseboat   "   "   ☆
When the Key Turned(Judd) Cupples -Syndicate
Dot and Dash in the Pumpkin Patch(West) Cupples   ☆
Clue in the Cobwebs(Keene) Grosset-Syndicate
In the Sunken Garden(Judd) Cupples-Syn icate   ☆
The Painted Shield(Wirt) Cupples   ☆
Ghost Gables (Wirt)   "   "   ☆
Danger at the Drawbridge(Wirt) Cupples
Mystery of the Brass Bound Trunk(Keene) Grosset-Syndicate
Honey Bunch-Her First Trip to a Big Fair Grosset-Syndicate
Behind the Green Dorr(Judd) Cupples-Syndicate
Dot and Dash at the Seashore(West) Cupples   ☆
Linda(Wirt) Cupples
Secret at the Gatehouse(Keene) Grosset-Syndicate
Flash Evans-Camera News Hawk (Bell)   Cupples   ☆
"   " and the Darkroom Mystery "   "   "   ☆
The Sacred Feather(Judd) Cupples-Syndicate
Mystery of the Laughing Mask(Wirt) Cupples
Mystery at the Moss Covered Mansion(Keene) Grosset-Syndicate
Honey Bunch;Her First Twin Playmates(Thorndyke) Grosset-Syndic ate   ☆
Clue of the Silken Ladder(Wirt) Cupples   ☆
The Secret Pact(Wirt)   Cupples
The Mysterious Fireplace(Keene) Grosset-Syndicate
Quest of the Missing Map(Keene)   "   "
The Clock Strikes Thirteen(Wirt) Cupples   ☆
The Wishing Well (Wirt) Cupples
Mystery of the Jewel Box(Keene) Grosset-Syndicate   ☆
Clue of the Rusty Key(Keene) Grosset-Syndicate
Portrait in the Sand(Keene) Grosset-Syndicate

Toledo Times
Toledo 4, Ohio

☆ = entirely Mildred A. Wirts ony even if written under pen name

3
Ghost Beyond the Gate(Wirt) Cupples   ☆
Saboteurs on the River (Wirt)   "   ☆
Hoofbeats on the Turnpike(Wirt) "   ☆
Secret in the Old Attic(Keene)   Grosset-Syndicate
Clue in the Crumbling Wall Keene)   "
Voice in the Cave   Wirt) Cupples   ☆
Signal in the Dark   (Wirt) Cupples   ☆
Clue of the Brass Thieves-(Keene) Grosset-Syndicate
Mystery of the Tolling Bell(Keene)   "   "
Whispering Walls (Wirt) Cupples   ☆
Secret of the Old Album(Keene) Grosset-Syndicate
Swamp Island(Wirt) Cupples   ☆
Cry at Midnight(Wirt) Cupples   ☆
Ghost of Blackwood Hall(Keene) Grosset-Syndicate
Pirate Brig(Scribner's   (Wirt)   ☆
Secret of the Jade Ring(Keene) Grosset-Syndicate
Clue in the Ivy- Keene-Grosset-Syndicate
Secret in the Old Well   "   "   ☆
Brownie Scouts at Snow Valley(Wirt) Cupples   ☆
"   "   at the Cherry Festival (Wirt) "   ☆
"   "   and Their Tree House   "   ☆
"   "   at Silver Beach   "   ☆
"   "   In the Circus   "   ☆
"   "   at the Tulip Festival(to be published)   ☆

Dan Carter-Cub Scout9 (Wirt) Cupples   ☆
"   "   and the River Camp "   ☆
"   "   and the Money Box "   ☆
"   "   and the Great Carved Face   "   ☆
"   "   and the Haunted Castle   "   ☆
"   "   and the Cub Honor   "(to be published)   ☆
Clue of the Rusty Key (Keene)   Grosset-Syndicate
Secret at the Gatehouse(Keene)   Grosset-Syndicate
Clue of the Velvet Mask(Keene) Grosset-Syndicate-to be
          published

Girl Scouts at Penguin Pass(Wirt)   Cupples   ☆
          (to be published
Girl Scouts at Calico Cave(Wirt)
          to be published-Cupples   ☆

Two Scout books-not titled   ☆ ☆

The Nancy Drew® Conference

Program

April 16 - 18, 1993

Iowa Memorial Union

THE UNIVERSITY OF IOWA

DURING THE NANCY DREW CONFERENCE, MILDRED WIRT BENSON WAS INTERVIEWED BY MEMBERS OF THE MEDIA

creating something that was an unusual book. I knew from the way that I felt when I wrote that it would be popular," she said.[3]

The conference put Millie on the map, and brought her the attention and recognition that she had never experienced before. Now the reporter was the one being asked the questions, and sometimes she wasn't too comfortable with it.

Thomas Walton, the editor of the *Blade* during Millie's last years, said, "As a reporter, as a journalist, she is not used to being the center of attention. She's used to writing about others. I think she's a little bit uncomfortable with the attention, but she recognizes that she gave America something special and, therefore, America wants to salute her back."[4]

Millie heard from many fans who told her what her characterization of Nancy Drew had meant to them. They wrote how Nancy Drew had inspired them to take on new challenges, to become independent, to become a success.

"I didn't think I was going to ever inspire anyone. I never dreamed that would be the result. I get lawyers and doctors and [people from] all walks of life, who say that I inspired them to be a success in their career. That's rather gratifying," Millie said.[5]

Women like Kate White, former editor-in-chief of *Cosmopolitan* magazine and a *New York Times* best-selling mystery writer, were inspired by Millie's characterization of Nancy. "I was a natural lover of books. While visiting my grandmother, in her parlor was a bookcase. *The Secret of the Red Gate Farm* stood out—it was like a beacon—with the image of Nancy peering behind the bushes. I remember thinking, 'Gosh that looks spooky. I want to know what the secret is.'"

Kate shared, "Here was this wonderful gutsy girl who had so much **autonomy**. I admired that sense of freedom that no one told Nancy what to do. It made me want to be a private detective. I bought this trench coat and had this little water pistol that I tucked in my pocket and pretended I was a private detective. Nancy Drew was imprinted in the most literal way with me. Over time she made me love mysteries and want to write mysteries. She made me fearless."[6]

Prolific adult and children's book author and winner of the prestigious Edgar Award, Dandi Daley Mackall, discovered Nancy Drew later in life.

"I grew up in a small Missouri town, where the library was in the basement of a bank and only open three afternoons a week and half of Saturday. The 'children's shelves' held fairy tales. And after that, books jumped to adults. So, when I should have been reading Nancy Drew, I was reading Agatha Christie," she said.

"It wasn't until I was grown up, writing mostly for adults, that I discovered Nancy Drew. My daughter Jen got hooked on the series . . . so I began reading Jen's books. I loved those stories! Each plot moved quickly, managing to create enough angst, while remaining safe and 'clean,'" she shared.

THE EDGARS

HAVE YOU discovered the writings of Edgar Allan Poe yet? The author of such favorites as "The Murders in the Rue Morgue," "The Mystery of Marie Rogêt," and "The Purloined Letter," Poe is considered the creator of the modern detective story. The Mystery Writers of America presents special awards, the Edgars, to the best mysteries published every year. Millie won a special Edgar award in 2001 in honor of her work on the Nancy Drew Mystery Stories. If you are looking for a good mystery to read, look into the Edgar award winners in the Juvenile category. Go to your local library or bookstore, grab your flashlight, and become a sleuth.

The salutes also came in the form of official recognition and tributes from organizations and institutions from throughout her life.

Millie had already received numerous awards for her writing. They included the Dodd, Mead Prize from *Boy's Life* in 1957 for her book, *Dangerous Deadline*, and the Amos Ives Root Award from the Ohio Aviation Trades Association for her articles on aviation. The Ohioana Library Association awarded her the Ohioana Citation for her contribution to children's literature in 1989.

Four years later, 1993 was a big year for her. For, on the heels of the Nancy Drew Conference, Millie was flooded with fan mail, requests to sign books, and more honors.

Millie was featured as the "Person of the Week" on ABC-TV's *World News Tonight*. Her adopted state of Ohio inducted her into the Ohio Women's Hall of Fame.

Thomas Walton accompanied Millie on the trip from Toledo to Columbus.

"I think she was the first one introduced . . . and, again, it gets back to the fact that many people didn't know the name Mildred Benson in 1993. But, as the governor was reading her life story and got to the point where he said that many of you know her better as Carolyn Keene, author of the original Nancy Drew, oh my gosh, it was like a wave of murmurs and you hear all these voices gathering and all of a sudden they all just rose as one in a standing ovation."

Millie was honored with the University of Iowa's Distinguished Alumni Award in June 1994 and inducted into the Iowa Women's Hall of Fame that August.[7]

In 1998 Millie once again accomplished a first. She was the first recipient of the *Blade*'s Lifetime Achievement Award for an Outstanding Journalist.

As Nancy Hawkins drove Millie to receive her Honorary Doctorate of Letters degree from Adrian College in 1999, they passed the airport Millie had flown out of on her many solo flights. Millie told Nancy a story about how she had a tough time landing her plane once, and slightly crashed. The gas tank began leaking. Millie scrambled out of the damaged plane. In pain, she tried to make it to the phone booth to call to get the plane towed out of there before the FAA (Federal Aviation Administration) showed up. Someone called the sheriff. The sheriff that came to look into the accident was smoking a cigarette, and Millie was very concerned about the gas leak and his cigarette. "I just had to get him out of there, was what she said," Nancy shared. So Millie told the sheriff she was just fine, and signed a form, and got the sheriff out of there.

Millie was a storyteller up until the very end.

Millie continued to work at the *Blade*, although she was forced, due to ailing health, to scale back to working one day a week. She wrote that, by being able to do so, "It will help me to stay in touch with my readers, my friends, and my life."[8]

A lifelong nonsmoker, Millie was diagnosed with lung cancer in June 1997. All those years of working in a smoke-filled newsroom had taken their toll. The day after her diagnosis, she was back at her desk, working. Millie was told she could go home. She replied, "This is where I need to be."[9]

Millie's last day was spent doing what she loved. Writing.

On Tuesday, May 28, 2002, she didn't feel well at work. She was taken home, and then, eventually, to a hospital. She died that evening.

Millie's life story was shared in obituary notices from coast to coast, including in the *New York Times* and the *Los Angeles Times*. Appropriately, her death made front-page news at the *Blade*. Her life story filled an entire page. Her final words, a piece written about the importance of the Carnegie libraries, appeared next to her obituary. At the end of her column, -30-, a journalism symbol that means the end of the story, was typed.[10]

Millie's chapters were filled with excitement, adventure, love, loss, and an indomitable spirit. Through it all she moved forward. In her little white shoes with blue laces when she was a toddler. Onto the athletic fields and diving platform at the University of Iowa. Into the office of a man creating books for young children. Up and away in airplanes. Up the steps of that federal district courthouse in 1980. Then, finally, she stepped out of our lives at the age of ninety-six.

"I've always been a person to think forward. You must think forward and not dwell on the past," Millie said.

Through her **storied** past we have solved the mystery of this tenacious ghostwriter, journalist, and adventurer. Perhaps now, given all the clues, Millie's entire life will serve as an inspiration to all of us well into the future.

-30-

EXTRA CLUES

Millie's Timeline

1905   *July 10:* Mildred (Millie) Lillian Augustine is born in Ladora, Iowa.

1922   *September:* Millie starts to attend classes at the University of Iowa, Iowa City.

1925   *June 9:* Millie obtains her undergraduate degree from the University of Iowa.

1925–26   Millie works as society editor for the *Clinton (IA) Herald*.

1926   *April 17:* Millie writes to the Stratemeyer Syndicate in response to an advertisement for writers.

      Summer: Millie travels to Europe with her parents, Lillian and J. L. Augustine.

      Millie meets with Edward Stratemeyer in New York City.

      September: Millie returns to the University of Iowa to obtain her masters degree.

      Millie meets Asa Alvin Wirt, an Associated Press telegraph operator and fellow student at the University of Iowa.

      October: Millie completes the manuscript of *Ruth Fielding and Her Great Scenario* for the Stratemeyer Syndicate.

1927   *June 6:* Millie is the first recipient of a Master of Arts degree from the University of Iowa School of Journalism.

1928   *March 4:* Millie and Asa Wirt are married in Chicago.

      Millie and Asa move to Cleveland.

1929   *October 3:* Edward Stratemeyer sends the outline for the first Nancy Drew mystery, *The Secret of the Old Clock*.

1930   Millie begins writing the Ruth Darrow Flying Series, her first series published under her own name.

April 28: The first three titles of the Nancy Drew Mystery Stories —its "breeder set"—are released.

May 10: Edward Stratemeyer dies.

Harriet and Edna Stratemeyer form a partnership to continue the Stratemeyer Syndicate operations.

1936   *November:* Margaret "Peggy" Wirt is born.

1938   Millie and Asa move to Toledo, Ohio.

1940   Millie and Asa move into home on Middlesex Drive, Toledo.

Asa Wirt has the first of a series of cerebral hemorrhages, or strokes.

1941   Asa Wirt takes leave of absence from Associated Press due to strokes.

1944   Millie begins work for the *Toledo Times.*

1947   *May 26:* Asa Wirt dies.

1950   *June 25:* Millie marries George Benson, the associate editor of the *Toledo Times.*

1953   Millie writes her last book for the Stratemeyer Syndicate.

1959   *February 27:* George Benson dies.

1967   Millie obtains her private pilot's license.

1971   Millie's mother, Lillian Augustine, dies.

1975   Millie becomes reporter for the *Toledo Blade* when the *Toledo Times* ceases operations.

1980   *May–June: Grosset & Dunlap vs. Gulf and Western (parent company of Simon and Schuster)* trial is held in the United States District Court, Southern District of New York, in Manhattan, New York City.

1993   *April 16–18:* The Nancy Drew Conference is held at the University of Iowa.

Millie is inducted into the Ohio Women's Hall of Fame.

1994   Millie is honored with Distinguished Alumni Award, University of Iowa.

Millie is inducted into the Iowa Women's Hall of Fame.

2002   *May 28:* Millie Benson dies in Toledo, Ohio.

Millie's Awards & Recognitions

1957 Boy's Life-Dodd, Mead Prize for *Dangerous Deadline*

1973 Amos Ives Root Award, Ohio Aviation Trades Association, for articles on aviation

1989 Ohioana Citation, Ohioana Library Association, for contribution to children's literature

1993 Honoree, Nancy Drew Conference, the University of Iowa
"Person of the Week," ABC-TV *World News Tonight*
Inducted into the Ohio Women's Hall of Fame

1994 Distinguished Alumni Achievement Award, the University of Iowa
Inducted into the Iowa Women's Hall of Fame

1997 Lifetime Achievement Award, Ohio Newspaper Women's Association

1998 First recipient, Lifetime Achievement Award for an Outstanding Journalist, the *Toledo Blade*

1999 Honorary Doctorate of Letters, Adrian College, Adrian, MI

2000 Touchstone Lifetime Achiever Award, Press Club of Toledo

2001 The Malice Domestic Award for Lifetime Achievement
Edgar Allan Poe Special Award, Mystery Writers of America

2002 Ohio Senior Citizens Hall of Fame

Millie's Chronological List of Works

based on year of publication, order within a series,
and alphabetical order by author, series, and title

1927   **RUTH FIELDING series** (RF)

       Ruth Fielding and Her Great Scenario
          Alice B. Emerson*

1928   *Ruth Fielding at Cameron Hall*
          Alice B. Emerson*

1929   *Ruth Fielding Clearing Her Name,*
          Alice B. Emerson*

1930   *Ruth Fielding in Talking Pictures*
          Alice B. Emerson*

       NANCY DREW MYSTERY STORIES (NDMS)

       The Secret of the Old Clock
       The Hidden Staircase
       The Bungalow Mystery
       The Mystery at Lilac Inn
          Carolyn Keene*

       RUTH DARROW FLYING STORIES (RDFS)

       Ruth Darrow in the Air Derby
       Ruth Darrow in the Fire Patrol
          Mildred A. Wirt

1931   **DORIS FORCE MYSTERY STORIES**
       Doris Force at Locked Gates
       Doris Force at Cloudy Cove
          Julia K. Duncan*

       Ruth Fielding and Baby June (RF)
          Alice B. Emerson*

*Stratemeyer Syndicate pseudonyms

The Secret at Shadow Ranch (NDMS)
The Secret of Red Gate Farm (NDMS)
   Carolyn Keene*

1932 *Ruth Fielding and Her Double* (RF)
       Alice B. Emerson*

      The Clue in the Diary (NDMS)
       Carolyn Keene*

MADGE STERLING series

The Missing Formula
The Deserted Yacht
The Secret of the Sundial
   Ann Wirt

1933 *Ruth Fielding and Her Greatest Triumph* (RF)
       Alice B. Emerson*

1934 *Ruth Fielding and Her Crowning Victory* (RF)
       Alice B. Emerson*

      The Clue of the Broken Locket (NDMS)
       Carolyn Keene*

1935 **A KAY TRACEY MYSTERY series** (KTM)

      The Mystery of the Swaying Curtains
      The Shadow on the Door
       Frances K. Judd*

      The Message in the Hollow Oak (NDMS)
       Carolyn Keene*

      Sky Racers
       Mildred A. Wirt

      THE MYSTERY STORIES FOR GIRLS** (TMSG)

      The Twin Ring Mystery
       Mildred A. Wirt

** These books were published by Cupples & Leon during the 1930s and featured stories by several authors, including Mildred A. Wirt. All of the books of this series were released as individual titles under an author's own name or pen name.

1936   PENNY NICHOLS MYSTERY SERIES (PNMS)

Penny Nichols Finds a Clue
Penny Nichols and the Mystery of the Lost Key
Penny Nichols and the Black Imp
     Joan Clark

The Six Fingered Glove Mystery (KTM)
The Green Cameo Mystery (KTM)
     Frances K. Judd*

DANA GIRLS MYSTERY STORIES (DGMS)

The Secret at the Hermitage
     Carolyn Keene*

The Mystery of the Ivory Charm (NDMS)
     Carolyn Keene*

Carolina Castle
     Mildred A. Wirt

MILDRED A. WIRT MYSTERY STORIES (MWMS)

The Clue at Crooked Lane
The Hollow Wall Mystery
     Mildred A. Wirt

1937   *The Secret at the Windmill* (KTM)
Beneath the Crimson Brier Bush (KTM)
     Frances K. Judd*

The Circle of Footprints (DGMS)
The Whispering Statue (NDMS)
The Haunted Bridge (NDMS)
     Carolyn Keene*

HONEY BUNCH BOOKS (HBB)

Honey Bunch: Her First Little Treasure Hunt
     Helen Louise Thorndyke*

Courageous Wings
The Shadow Stone (MWMS)
     Mildred A. Wirt

TRAILER STORIES FOR GIRLS (TSG)

The Runaway Caravan
The Crimson Cruiser
Timbered Treasure
    Mildred A. Wirt

1938   *The Message in the Sand Dunes* (KTM)
    The Murmuring Portrait (KTM)
       Frances K. Judd*

    The Mystery of the Locked Room (DGMS)
       Carolyn Keene*

    Honey Bunch: Her First Little Club (HBB)
       Helen Louise Thorndyke*

DOT AND DASH SERIES (D&DS)

Dot and Dash at the Maple Sugar Camp
Dot and Dash at Happy Hollow
Dot and Dash in the North Woods
    Dorothy West

The Wooden Shoe Mystery (MWMS)
Through the Moon-Gate Door (MWMS)
The Phantom Trailer (TSG)
    Mildred A. Wirt

1939   *Penny Nichols and the Knob Hill Mystery* (PNMS)
    Connie Carl at Rainbow Ranch
       Joan Clark

    When the Key Turned (KTM)
    In the Sunken Garden (KTM)
       Frances K. Judd*

    The Clue in the Cobweb (DGMS)
    The Clue of the Tapping Heels (NDMS)
       Carolyn Keene*

    Honey Bunch: Her First Trip in a Trailer (HBB)
       Helen Louise Thorndyke*

Dot and Dash in the Pumpkin Patch (D&DS)
    Dorothy West

Ghost Gables (MWMS)
The Painted Shield (MWMS)
    Mildred A. Wirt

PENNY PARKER MYSTERY STORIES (PPMS)
Tale of the Witch Doll
The Vanishing Houseboat
    Mildred A. Wirt

1940 **FLASH EVANS BOOKS**
Flash Evans and the Darkroom Mystery
Flash Evans, Camera News Hawk
    Frank Bell

The Sacred Feather (KTM)
    Frances K. Judd*

The Secret at the Gatehouse (DGMS)
The Mystery of the Brass Bound Trunk (NDMS)
    Carolyn Keene*

Honey Bunch: Her First Trip to a Big Fair (HBB)
    Helen Louise Thorndyke*

Dot and Dash at the Seashore (D&DS)
    Dorothy West

Linda
Danger at the Drawbridge (PPMS)
Behind the Green Door (PPMS)
Mystery of the Laughing Mask (TMSG)
    Mildred A. Wirt

1941 *The Mysterious Fireplace* (DGMS)
The Mystery at the Moss-Covered Mansion (NDMS)
    Carolyn Keene*

Honey Bunch: Her First Twin Playmates (HBB)
    Helen Louise Thorndyke*

Clue of the Silken Ladder (PPMS)
The Secret Pact (PPMS)
   Mildred A. Wirt

1942 *Mystery at the Lookout*
The Clue of the Rusty Key (DGMS)
The Quest of the Missing Map (NDMS)
   Carolyn Keene*

The Clock Strikes Thirteen (PPMS)
The Wishing Well (PPMS)
   Mildred A. Wirt

1943 *The Portrait in the Sand* (DGMS)
The Clue in the Jewel Box (NDMS)
   Carolyn Keene*

Ghost Beyond the Gate (PPMS)
Saboteurs on the River (PPMS)
   Mildred A. Wirt

1944 *The Secret in the Old Well* (DGMS)
The Secret in the Old Attic (NDMS)
   Carolyn Keene*

Hoofbeats on the Turnpike (PPMS)
Voice from the Cave (PPMS)
   Mildred A. Wirt

1945 *The Clue in the Crumbling Wall* (NDMS)
   Carolyn Keene*

Guilt of the Brass Thieves (PPMS)
   Mildred A. Wirt

1946 *The Mystery of the Tolling Bell* (NDMS)
   Carolyn Keene*

Signal in the Dark (PPMS)
Whispering Walls (PPMS)
   Mildred A. Wirt

1947   *The Clue in the Old Album* (NDMS)
        Carolyn Keene*

        Swamp Island (PPMS)
        The Cry at Midnight (PPMS)
        Mildred A. Wirt

1948   *The Ghost of Blackwood Hall* (NDMS)
        Carolyn Keene*

1949   **BROWNIE SCOUT SERIES** (BSS)

        The Brownie Scouts at Snow Valley
        The Brownie Scouts in the Circus
        Mildred A. Wirt

        DAN CARTER SERIES (DCS)

        Dan Carter, Cub Scout
        Dan Carter and the River Camp
        Mildred A. Wirt

1950   *Pirate Brig*
        The Brownie Scouts in the Cherry Festival (BSS)
        Dan Carter and the Money Box (DCS)
        Mildred A. Wirt

1951   *The Brownie Scouts and Their Tree House* (BSS)
        Dan Carter and the Haunted Castle (DCS)
        Mildred A. Wirt

1952   *The Clue in the Ivy* (DGMS)
        Carolyn Keene*

        The Brownie Scouts at Silver Beach (BSS)
        Dan Carter and the Great Carved Face (DCS)
        Mildred A. Wirt

1953   *The Secret of the Jade Ring* (DGMS)
        The Clue of the Velvet Mask (NDMS)
        Carolyn Keene*

The Brownie Scouts at Windmill Farm (BSS)
Dan Carter and the Cub Honor (DCS)
   Mildred A. Wirt

THE GIRL SCOUT SERIES (GSS)
The Girl Scouts at Penguin Pass
   Mildred A. Wirt

1954 *Mystery at the Crossroads* (DGMS)
     Carolyn Keene*

1955 **THE BOY SCOUT EXPLORER SERIES** (BSES)
     The Boy Scout Explorers at Emerald Valley
     The Boy Scout Explorers at Treasure Mountain
       Don Palmer

     The Girl Scouts at Singing Sands (GSS)
       Mildred A. Wirt

1957 *Dangerous Deadline*
     Mildred Benson

     The Boy Scout Explorers at Headless Hollow (BSES)
       Don Palmer

     The Girl Scouts at Mystery Mansion (GSS)
       Mildred A. Wirt

1959 *Quarry Ghost*
     (published in the United Kingdom as *Kristie at College*, 1960)
     Mildred Benson

Glossary

alma mater: College or university from which an individual has graduated

alumni: Former students of a college or university

autonomy: Independence or freedom

aviatrix: Female pilot

beat: Reporter's routine covering of the same news sources

bush pilots: Pilots that transport individuals or cargo to remote areas of the world

byline: In a newspaper, the line naming the writer of a story

epitaph: Short text honoring a deceased person on his or her tombstone

familiarization: Process of making known, of gaining knowledge about something

feature: Nonfiction newspaper or magazine story intended primarily to entertain or instruct

freelance writer: Writer who is self-employed and not contracted with a newspaper or publication

Gallup Poll: Statistical method of determining public opinion by surveying a representative sample of persons

ghostwriter: Someone who writes for, and in the name of, another person

lead: First paragraph of a story, written in a style both to pull the reader into the story and to set the story's tone

lucrative: Producing a great deal of profit

mercantile: General store, one selling a wide variety of goods

nom de plume: Pen name; fictitious name by which an author is known

parent company: Company that owns enough shares of stock in another business to control votes determining its management and operations

penchant: Strong liking for something or tendency to do something

press conference: Media event where newsmakers invite journalists to hear them speak and ask questions

prolific: Creating works in abundance

protagonists: Main characters of a story

pseudonym: Fictitious name used by an author or artist

ratified: Formally approved and made valid

repertoire: Range of skills or special accomplishments of a person

roadster: Term for a sporty automobile

royalty: In publishing, a payment made to the owner of the copyright or to the author of a piece for each sale or use of the written work

scenario: Written outline of a movie, book, or play giving details of the plot, characters, and specific scenes

sidebar: Short news story or graphic accompanying a longer newspaper or magazine article

statistics: Facts or data from a study of a large amount of numerical data

storied: Celebrated in story; having an interesting history

story papers: Weekly inexpensive publications of action-packed serial stories, featuring cliffhanger endings and plots that continued through several issues

syndicate: Group of individuals formed to transact a specific business

thesis: Document submitted by a student toward obtaining a master's degree, presenting his or her research

thrombosis: Formation or presence of a blood clot in a vein or artery

Tiffany: Artwork—including vases, lamps, mosaics, and stained glass—created by Louis Comfort Tiffany

turbulence: Violent or unsteady movement of air or water

undergraduate: Post-secondary education; years of education following high school and including all levels up to a bachelor's degree

writing credits: Body of work by a writer

Acknowledgments

THERE IS a whole cast of characters who lent their time and expertise to solving the mysteries of Mildred Augustine Wirt Benson's life. They are, based on order of appearance in the process, the following:

Brad, Kyle, and Ian Rubini. Without their support to follow this trail to where it might take me, you would not be reading this. I love them all dearly.

Michelle Houts. She offered guidance all along the way.

The staff of Ohio University Press who brought Millie's story to light.

Geoffrey S. Lapin. He was an avid supporter and dear friend to Millie.

Thomas Walton. He put some of the first clues together for me, and made sure they were presented clearly.

Leslee Hooper, Nancy Eames, Michael Lora, Jill Clever, and the staff of the Local History & Genealogy Department at the Toledo-Lucas County Public Library. They helped me solve several mysteries along the way.

With special thanks to WGTE Public Media, producer of the television documentary *The Storied Life of Millie Benson,* for their invaluable assistance. As I never had the chance to meet Millie, the documentary's extensive footage provided insights into her character.

Karen Mason and Carolyn Stewart Dyer were very gracious and served as amazing resources at the Iowa Women's Archives of the University of Iowa Libraries. So, too, did David McCartney of the University of Iowa Archives. Without the permissions granted by the Mildred Wirt Benson Papers, the Iowa Women's Archives, the University of Iowa Libraries, and the University of Iowa, this project would not be as complete.

Lois Kovar and Kay Morgan sat with me in Millie's childhood home and shared keepsakes, photos, and memories that were invaluable. I appreciate their trust.

The staff of the State of Iowa Historical Society.

Marilyn Rogers of the Pioneer Heritage Resource Library was invaluable in providing records, articles, and photos.

The staff at the Stratemeyer Syndicate Archives of The New York Public Library. You rock.

David Ng of United States District Court, Southern District of New York.

I admire Jenn Fisher's passion for Nancy Drew, and appreciate her willingness to meet with me.

Nancy Hawkins, friend and confidant of Millie. I appreciate her honesty, hospitality, and insight.

James E. Keeline, Stratemeyer Syndicate authority and author. A huge thanks for his time, research, and review of the manuscript.

The *Toledo Blade* for the cooperation of its staff and the newspaper's permission to share Millie's articles and images.

I also appreciate the assistance of author Henry M. Holden; Francesca Pitaro, archivist with AP; Verna at the Palmer House Hotel; Bill Huber of Huber Photography; and the staff at the Federal Aviation Administration.

Most of all, thank you to Mildred Augustine Wirt Benson for serving as an inspiration to us all.

Notes

The First Clue: Ghostwriter Reappears

1. James Keeline, written correspondence, May 28, 2015.
2. Deidre Johnson, *Edward Stratemeyer and the Stratemeyer Syndicate* (New York: Twayne Publishers, 1993), 6.
3. Melanie Rehak, *Girl Sleuth: Nancy Drew and the Women Who Created Her* (Orlando, FL: Harcourt, 2005), 25.
4. Deidre Johnson, "From Paragraphs to Pages: The Writing and Development of the Stratemeyer Syndicate Series," *Rediscovering Nancy Drew* (Iowa City: University of Iowa Press, 1995), 29.
5. Johnson, *Edward Stratemeyer*, 33.
6. Geoffrey S. Lapin, "The Ghost of Nancy Drew," *Books at Iowa 50*, (Iowa City: Friends of the University of Iowa Libraries, April 1989), 21.
7. People, *Time*, April 28, 1980.
8. Rehak, *Girl Sleuth*, 294.
9. Johnson. *Edward Stratemeyer*, 3.
10. Ibid., 6.
11. *Grosset & Dunlap vs. Gulf and Western Corporation and Stratemeyer Syndicate* 79 Civ. 2242, 367, May 27, 1980.
12. Geoffrey S. Lapin, telephone interview, December 28, 2013.
13. Lapin, "The Ghost of Nancy Drew," 21.
14. James E. Keeline, "The Nancy Drew Mythtery Stories," *Nancy Drew and Her Sister Sleuths.* Jefferson, NC: McFarland & Company, 2008.

The Second Clue: Little Ladora Girl with Big Dreams

1. Jeanne Maglaty, "When Did Girls Start Wearing Pink?," Smithsonian .com, April 7, 2011.

2. James C. Dinwiddie, *History of Iowa County, Iowa, and Its People,* vol. 2 (Chicago: The S. J. Clarke Publishing Company, 1915), 38.

3. Ibid., 39.

4. Lois Kovar (great-niece) and Kay Morgan (niece), personal interview, March 26, 2014, in Ladora, IA.

5. *The Storied Life of Millie Benson,* Gregory Tye, producer, WGTE Public Media, November 9, 1999.

6. Mildred Wirt Benson, "Paper dolls, spools were early props in a child's attempts at storytelling," *Toledo Blade,* June 9, 2001, sec. D, 1.

7. Lois Kovar and Kay Morgan, interview.

8. *The Storied Life of Millie Benson.*

9. Ibid.

10. Ibid.

11. Susan R. Gannon, Suzanne Rahn, and Ruth Anne Thompson, eds. *St. Nicholas and Mary Mapes Dodge: The Legacy of a Children's Magazine Editor, 1873–1905* (Jefferson, NC: McFarland & Co., Inc., 2004), 9.

12. *The Storied Life of Millie Benson.*

13. Ibid.

14. Rehak, *Girl Sleuth,* 46.

15. Dave Rasdal, "Ladora girl grew up to be Nancy Drew creator," *Cedar Rapids Gazette,* Sunday, September 19, 1999, Iowa Women's Archives, the University of Iowa Libraries.

The Third Clue: College Days

1. Scrapbook created by Lillian Augustine for Mildred.

2. David McCartney, "Old Gold. What's in a name? For The University of Iowa lots of history and a little confusion," University of Iowa *Spectator,* December 2010. The official name of the University of Iowa was the State University of Iowa, although the university was often referred to by its unofficial name. In October 1964, the university Board of Regents approved using "University of Iowa" for everyday use.

3. School of Journalism & Mass Communication, College of Arts and Sciences, University of Iowa, http://clas.uiowa.edu/sjmc/.

4. State University of Iowa *Directory,* 1922–23, Class C I6HI, Acc 4177, 27.

5. Old Capitol Museum, University of Iowa, http://www.uiowa.edu/~oldcap/history.shtml.

6. John C. Gerber, with Carolyn B. Brown, James Kaufmann, and James B. Lindberg Jr., *A Pictorial History of the University of Iowa* (Iowa City: University of Iowa Press, 1988), 148.

7. Personal scrapbook, Iowa Women's Archives, the University of Iowa Libraries, box 2.

8. Gerber, *A Pictorial History of the University of Iowa*, 125.

9. State University of Iowa, Schedule of Courses, 1924–25.

10. The Iowa *Alumnus,* vol. 18, October 1920–June 1921, University of Iowa, 76.

11. Everett M. Rogers, *A History of Communication Study: A Biographical Approach* (New York: The Free Press, 1994), excerpted online at http://catdir .loc.gov/catdir/samples/simon052/93043281.html.

12. Richard Reeves, "George Gallup's Nation of Numbers," *Esquire,* December 1983, 91–92.

13. The *Daily Iowan,* June 13, 1925, 1.

The Fourth Clue: Next Steps

1. "The Newarker who is best known," *Newark Sunday Call,* December 9, 1917.

2. J. Randolph Cox, *The Dime Novel Companion: A Source Book* (Westport, CT: Greenwood Press, 2000), xiii.

3. Letter and advertisement from the editor, Stratemeyer Syndicate Records, New York Public Library, box 16, files E, R.

4. Letter from Mildred Augustine to Stratemeyer Syndicate, April 21, 1926, Stratemeyer Syndicate Records, New York Public Library, box 14, file A, 1925–27.

5. Letter from Harriet Otis Smith to Mildred Augustine, April 21, 1926, Stratemeyer Syndicate Records, New York Public Library, box 43, file "correspondence with Mildred Benson, 1926–1931."

6. Letter from Edward Stratemeyer to Mildred Augustine, May 10, 1926, Stratemeyer Syndicate Records, New York Public Library, box 26.

7. Lois Kovar and Kay Morgan, interview.

8. Scrapbook created by Lillian Augustine for Mildred.

9. Ancestry.com, passenger list from RMS *Andania II,* U.S. Department of Labor list of United States citizens.

The Fifth Clue: New Name, New Character, New Beginning

1. Alice B. Emerson, *Ruth Fielding and Her Great Scenario* (New York: Cupples & Leon Co., 1927), 1.

2. Ibid., 12.

3. Mildred Wirt Benson, "The Ghost of Ladora," *Books at Iowa 19* (Iowa City: Friends of the University of Iowa Libraries, November 1973), 25.

4. Letter from Edward Stratemeyer to Mildred Augustine, October 29, 1926, Stratemeyer Syndicate Records, New York Public Library, box 44.

5. Emerson, *Ruth Fielding*, 11.

6. Ibid., 64.

7. Ibid., 73.

8. "Thrills Everyday Occurrence for Associated Press Wire Operators of *Post-Telegram*," *Bridgeport Post-Telegram*, July 26, 1925, 4.

9. Heidi Anderson, "Wirespeak: a brief look at an even briefer language," *AP World*, Jan–Feb. 1993.

10. Benson, "The Ghost of Ladora," 25.

11. *Daily Iowan*, June 5, 1927, 5.

12. Wallace Rice, *Palmer House, Old and New: An Historical Sketch with Reminiscences of Chicago Two Generations Ago, Together with a Description of the Palmer House Today* (Chicago: The Chicago Hotel Company, 1925), 9.

13. Personal scrapbook, Iowa Women's Archives, the University of Iowa Libraries.

14. Claudia Goldin, "The work and wages of single women, 1870–1920," *Journal of Economic History*, vol. 40, no. 1 (Cambridge: Cambridge University Press, March 1980), 81–88.

15. Rehak, *Girl Sleuth*, 111. Letter from Mildred Wirt to Edward Stratemeyer, May 16, 1928, Stratemeyer Syndicate Records, New York Public Library, box 117.

16. Recipe courtesy of the Palmer House Hilton Hotel, Chicago. Variations on this recipe are available at http://lostrecipesfound.com/recipe/the-palmer -house-hilton-original-chocolate-fudge-brownie/ and http://www.chocolateatlas .com/Chocolate_Recipes/S001_Chocolate_Fudge_brownie.htm.

The Sixth Clue: Nancy Drew

1. Johnson, "From Paragraphs to Pages," 29.

2. Keeline, "The Nancy Drew Mythtery Stories."

3. Johnson, *Edward Stratemeyer*, 7.

4. Carole Kismaric and Marvin Heiferman, *The Mysterious Case of Nancy Drew and the Hardy Boys* (New York: Simon & Schuster, 1998), 16.

5. Carolyn Keene, *The Secret of the Old Clock* (New York: Grosset & Dunlap, 1930), 76.

6. Letter from Edward Stratemeyer to Mildred A. Wirt, November 8, 1929, Stratemeyer Syndicate Records, New York Public Library.

7. *The Storied Life of Millie Benson,* outtakes, tape #6.

8. Letter from Edward Stratemeyer to Mildred A. Wirt, December 3, 1929, Stratemeyer Syndicate Records, New York Public Library (on display in exhibit while conducting research).

9. Marilyn S. Greenwald, *The Secret of the Hardy Boys: Leslie McFarlane and the Stratemeyer Syndicate* (Athens: Ohio University Press, 2004), 93.

10. Rehak, *Girl Sleuth,* 123.

11. History cable channel, www.history.com/topics.great-depression.

12. Letter from Mildred A. Wirt to Edward Stratemeyer April 30, 1930, Stratemeyer Syndicate Records, New York Public Library.

13. Cox, *The Dime Novel Companion,* 252.

14. Rehak, *Girl Sleuth,* 140.

15. Ibid., 169.

The Seventh Clue: Different Characters/Similar Lives

1. *New York Times,* May 2, 1930, 1.

2. Letter from Mildred A. Wirt to Harriet Otis Smith, Stratemeyer Syndicate Records, New York Public Library.

3. Lapin, "The Ghost of Nancy Drew," 9.

4. Julie Cummins, *Flying Solo: How Ruth Elder Soared into America's Heart* (New York: Roaring Book Press, 2013), author's note.

5. Joan Clark, *Penny Nichols Finds A Clue* (Chicago: Goldsmith Publishing Co, 1936).

6. *The Storied Life of Millie Benson.*

7. Letter from Mildred A. Wirt to Edna Stratemeyer, January 10, 1937, Stratemeyer Syndicate Records, New York Public Library, box 44.

8. Letter from Edna Stratemeyer to Mildred A. Wirt, January 21, 1937, Stratemeyer Syndicate Records, New York Public Library, box 44.

9. Gene Nora Jessen, *The Powder Puff Derby of 1929: The True Story of the First Women's Cross-Country Air Race* (Naperville, IL: Sourcebooks, Inc., 2002), xiv.

10. Jessen, *Powder Puff Derby*, 66.
11. Ibid., 199.

The Eighth Clue: Sad Loss & New Beginning

1. Letter from Mildred A. Wirt to Edna Stratemeyer Squier, January 4, 1941, Stratemeyer Syndicate Records, New York Public Library, box 44.
2. Letter from Mildred A. Wirt to Harriet Stratemeyer Adams, May 1, 1942, Stratemeyer Syndicate Records, New York Public Library, box 44.
3. Asa Alvin Wirt treasury card, Associated Press corporate archives.
4. Letter from Mildred A. Wirt to Harriet Stratemeyer Adams, July 18, 1944, Stratemeyer Syndicate Records, New York Public Library, box 44.
5. Rehak, *Girl Sleuth*, 215.
6. *The Storied Life of Millie Benson.*
7. Mildred A. Wirt, "Toledo Aviatrix Taught Fliers Around Globe Their First 'Steps,'" *Toledo Times*, March 19, 1945.
8. Letter from Mildred A. Wirt to Harriet Stratemeyer Adams, May 5, 1947, Stratemeyer Syndicate Records, New York Public Library, box 44.
9. Rehak, *Girl Sleuth*, 223.
10. Letter from Mildred A. Wirt to Harriet Stratemeyer Adams, June 22, 1947, Stratemeyer Syndicate Records, New York Public Library, box 44.
11. Letter from Mildred A. Wirt Benson to Harriet Stratemeyer Adams, July 17, 1951, Stratemeyer Syndicate Records, New York Public Library, box 44.
12. Lois Kovar and Kay Morgan, interview.
13. Rehak, *Girl Sleuth*, 235.

The Ninth Clue: Take Off!

1. Mildred Wirt Benson, flight log book, 1965.
2. *Toledo Times*, February 28, 1957, 7.
3. Mildred Wirt Benson, "Happy Landings First Ride, in a Jenny, Led My Way to Flight," *Toledo Blade*, December 13, 1970, sec. G, 2.
4. *The Storied Life of Millie Benson*, tape #7.
5. Lawrence Keeler, NASA journalist-in-space application essay on behalf of Mildred Benson, January 5, 1986.
6. Federal Aviation Administration. www.faa.gov/licenses_certificates/.
7. Federal Aviation Administration, correspondence with, August 11, 2014.

The Final Clues: Nancy Drew Conference,
Recognition & Legacy

1. The Nancy Drew Conference, program introduction, 2.

2. *The Storied Life of Millie Benson.*

3. Ibid.

4. Ibid.

5. Ibid.

6. Kate White, telephone interview, July 14, 2014.

7. Iowa Women's Archives, the University of Iowa Libraries, http://sdrc .lib.uiowa.edu/iwa/findingaids/html/BensonMildred.htm.

8. Mildred Wirt Benson, "Millie Benson's Notebook," *Toledo Blade*, December 29, 2001, sec. D, 8.

9. Mark Zaborney and George J. Tanber, "*Blade* columnist, Nancy Drew author Millie Benson dies at 96," *Toledo Blade*, May 29, 2002, sec. A, 4.

10. Rose Russell, "A Life Well Lived," *Toledo Blade*, Pages of Opinion, May 21, 2002.

Bibliography

Books

Clark, Joan. *See* Wirt, Mildred A.

Cornelius, Michael G., and Melanie E. Gregg, eds. *Nancy Drew and Her Sister Sleuths.* Jefferson, NC: McFarland & Company, Inc., 2008.

Cox, J. Randolph. *The Dime Novel Companion: A Source Book.* Westport, CT: Greenwood Press, 2000.

Cummins, Julie. *Flying Solo: How Ruth Elder Soared into America's Heart.* New York: Roaring Book Press, 2013.

Dinwiddie, James C. *History of Iowa County, Iowa, and Its People.* Vol. 2. Chicago: The S. J. Clarke Publishing Co., 1915.

Duncan, Julia K. *See* Wirt, Mildred A.

Dyer, Carolyn Stewart, and Nancy Tillman Romalov, eds. *Rediscovering Nancy Drew.* Iowa City: University of Iowa Press, 1995.

Emerson, Alice B. *See* Wirt, Mildred A.

Gannon, Susan R., Suzanne Rahn, and Ruth Anne Thompson, eds. *St. Nicholas and Mary Mapes Dodge: The Legacy of a Children's Magazine Editor, 1873–1905.* Jefferson, NC: McFarland & Company, Inc., 2004.

Gerber, John C., with Carolyn B. Brown, James Kaufmann, and James B. Lindberg Jr. *A Pictorial History of The University of Iowa.* Iowa City: University of Iowa Press, 1988.

Greenwald, Marilyn S. *The Secret of the Hardy Boys: Leslie McFarlane and the Stratemeyer Syndicate.* Athens: Ohio University Press, 2004.

Jessen, Gene Nora. *The Powder Puff Derby of 1929: The True Story of the First Women's Cross-Country Air Race.* Naperville, IL: Sourcebooks, Inc., 2002.

Johnson, Deidre. *Edward Stratemeyer and the Stratemeyer Syndicate.* New York: Twayne Publishers, 1993.

Judd, Frances K. *See* Wirt, Mildred A.

Kasson, John F. *The Little Girl Who Fought the Great Depression: Shirley Temple and 1930s America.* New York: W. W. Norton and Company, 2014.

Keene, Carolyn. *See* Wirt, Mildred A.

Kismaric, Carole, and Marvin Heiferman. *The Mysterious Case of Nancy Drew and the Hardy Boys.* New York: Simon & Schuster, 1998.

Plunkett-Powell, Karen. *The Nancy Drew Scrapbook.* New York: St. Martin's Press, 1993.

Rehak, Melanie. *Girl Sleuth: Nancy Drew and the Women Who Created Her.* Orlando, FL: Harcourt Press, 2005.

Rice, Wallace. *Palmer House, Old and New: An Historical Sketch with Reminiscences of Chicago Two Generations Ago, Together with a Description of the Palmer House Today.* Chicago: The Chicago Hotel Company, 1925.

Rogers, Everett M. *A History of Communication Study: A Biographical Approach.* New York: The Free Press, 1994. Excerpted online at http://catdir .loc.gov/catdir/samples/simon052/93043281.html.

Wirt, Ann. *See* Wirt, Mildred A.

Wirt, Mildred A. *Ruth Darrow in the Air Derby, Or Recovering the Silver Trophy.* New York: Barse & Company, 1930.

———. *The Clue at Crooked Lane.* New York: Cupples & Leon, 1936.

———. [Joan Clark, pseud.]. *Penny Nichols Finds a Clue.* Chicago: Goldsmith Publishing Co., 1936.

———. [Julia K. Duncan, pseud.]. *Doris Force at Locked Gates.* Chicago: Goldsmith Publishing Company, 1931.

———. [Alice B. Emerson, pseud.]. *Ruth Fielding and Her Great Scenario.* New York: Cupples & Leon Company, 1927.

———. [Frances K. Judd, pseud.]. *The Mystery of the Swaying Curtains.* New York: Cupples & Leon, 1935.

———. [Carolyn Keene, pseud.]. *The Secret of the Old Clock.* New York: Grosset & Dunlap, 1930.

———. [Ann Wirt, pseud.]. *The Missing Formula.* Chicago: Goldsmith Publishing Company, 1932.

Essays

Benson, Mildred Wirt. "The Ghost of Ladora." *Books at Iowa 19.* Iowa City: Friends of the University of Iowa Libraries, November 1973.

Lapin, Geoffrey S. "The Ghost of Nancy Drew." *Books at Iowa 50.* Iowa City: Friends of the University of Iowa Libraries, April 1989. Reprinted in *Library Literature 20: The Best of 1989.* Metuchen, NJ: Scarecrow Press, 1991.

Johnson, Deidre. "From Paragraphs to Pages: The Writing and Development of the Stratemeyer Syndicate Series." *Rediscovering Nancy Drew*. Iowa City: University of Iowa Press, 1995.

Keeline, James D. "The Nancy Drew Mythtery Stories." *Nancy Drew and Her Sister Sleuths*. Jefferson, NC: McFarland & Company, 2008.

Karell, Linda K. "Originator, Writer, Editor, Hack: Carolyn Keene and Changing Definitions of Authorship." *Nancy Drew and Her Sister Sleuths*. Jefferson, NC: McFarland & Company, 2008.

Articles

Anderson, Heidi. "Wirespeak: A brief look at an even briefer language." *AP World*, January–February 1993.

Benson, Mildred Wirt. "Happy Landings: First Ride, in a Jenny, Led My Way to Flight." *Toledo Blade*, December 13, 1970, sec. G, 2.

———. "Millie Benson's Notebook." *Toledo Blade*, December 29, 2001, sec. D, 8.

———. "Paper dolls, spools were early props in a child's attempts at storytelling." *Toledo Blade*, June 9, 2001, sec. D, 1.

———. *See also* Wirt, Mildred A.

Borelli, Christopher. "ABC morning show gets an earful from *The Blade*'s Benson." *Toledo Blade*, October 14, 1998.

Davis, Parke H. "Expert Football for the Spectator or, How to Watch a Football Game as an Expert Watches It." *St. Nicholas for Boys and Girls*. Volume XLIV, November 1916–April 1917.

Goldin, Claudia. "The Work and Wages of Single Women, 1870–1920." *Journal of Economic History* 40, no. 1. (March 1980).

Maglaty, Jeanne. "When Did Girls Start Wearing Pink?" *Smithsonian.com*, April 7, 2011.

McCartney, David. "Old Gold. What's in a name? For The University of Iowa lots of history and a little confusion." University of Iowa *Spectator*, December 2010.

Rasdal, Dave. "Ladora girl grew up to be Nancy Drew creator." *Cedar Rapids Gazette*, September 19, 1999.

Reeves, Richard. "George Gallup's Nation of Numbers." *Esquire*, December 1983.

Russell, Rose. "A Life Well Lived." *Toledo Blade*, May 21, 2002, Pages of Opinion.

"The Newarker who is best known." *Newark Sunday Call,* December 19, 1917.

"Thrills Everyday Occurrence for Associated Press Wire Operators of *Post-Telegram.*" *Bridgeport Post-Telegram,* July 26, 1925, 4.

Time. People. April 28, 1980.

Vallongo, Sally. "Thoroughly Marvelous Millie: Writer Millie Benson winds down her astonishing career." *Toledo Blade,* December 23, 2001, sec. E, 1.

Wirt, Mildred A. "Toledo Aviatrix Taught Fliers Around Globe Their First 'Steps.'" *Toledo Times,* March 19, 1945.

Zaborney, Mark, and George J. Tanber. "*Blade* columnist, Nancy Drew Author Millie Benson dies at 96." *Toledo Blade,* May 29, 2002, sec. A, 4.

Websites

Ancestry.com.

Chocolate Atlas. http://www.chocolateatlas.com/Chocolate_Recipes/S001_Chocolate_Fudge_brownie.htm.

Federal Aviation Administration. www.faa.gov/licenses_certificates/.

History cable channel. www.history.com.

Lost Recipes Found. http://lostrecipesfound.com/recipe/the-palmer-house-hilton-original-chocolate-fudge-brownie/.

The Ninety-Nines, Inc., International Organization of Women Pilots. www.ninety-nines.org.

University of Iowa. www.uiowa.edu.

Film

Incorporating excerpts from *The Storied Life of Millie Benson,* Gregory Tye, producer, WGTE Public Media, November 9, 1999.

Interviews

Fisher, Jennifer. April 24, 2014.

Hawkins, Nancy. April 27, 2014.

Keeline, James. April 28, 2014.

Kovar, Lois, and Kay Morgan. March 26, 2014.

Lapin, Geoffrey S. Telephone interview, December 28, 2013.
Mackall, Dandi Daley. E-mail correspondence, July 24, 2014.
Mason, Karen, and Carolyn Stewart Dyer. March 11, 2014.
Walton, Thomas. March 6, 2014.
White, Kate. Telephone interview. July 14, 2014.

Additional Resources

In addition to the resources above, the author was granted access to the following archives:

Associated Press corporate archives.

Iowa Women's Archives, the University of Iowa Libraries.

Stratemeyer Syndicate Records; Manuscripts and Archives Division; The New York Public Library; Astor, Lenox, and Tilden Foundations.

The Blade Rare Book Room, Local History & Genealogy Department, Toledo-Lucas County Public Library.

Millie's family provided the author with keepsakes, photographs, and wonderful memories.

These archives included personal correspondence, photographs, notes, and souvenirs. Several of the scrapbooks included clippings from newspapers including the *Daily Iowan*, the *Cleveland Plain Dealer*, the *Toledo Times*, and the *Toledo Blade*.

Millie's early travel information was confirmed through Ancestry.org. Her family information was confirmed through Familysearch.org.